RETURN TO SENDER

Houghton Mifflin Company 1975 Boston

RAYMOND MUNGO

OR

When The Fish In The Water Was Thirsty

A San Francisco Book Company/Houghton Mifflin Book

Library of Congress Cataloging in Publication Data

Mungo, Raymond, 1946-
Return to sender.
"A San Francisco Book Company/Houghton Mifflin book."
1. Asia — Description and travel — 1951-
2. Mungo, Raymond, 1946-   I. Title.
II. Title: When the fish in the water was thirsty.
DS10.M78   915'.04'420924   75-12661
ISBN 0-395-20505-0   ISBN 0-913374-24-5

This SAN FRANCISCO BOOK
COMPANY / HOUGHTON MIFFLIN
BOOK originated in San Francisco and
was produced and published jointly.
Distribution is by Houghton Mifflin
Company, 2 Park Street, Boston,
Massachusetts 02107.

I laugh when I hear the fish in the water is thirsty.
You do not yet see that the Real is in your own home,
And you wander from forest to forest listlessly.
Here is the truth! Go where you will, to Banaras or to
Mathura,
If you do not find god in your own soul
The world will be meaningless to you.

—KABIR

For D.L., AZUL, *and* PHOENIX

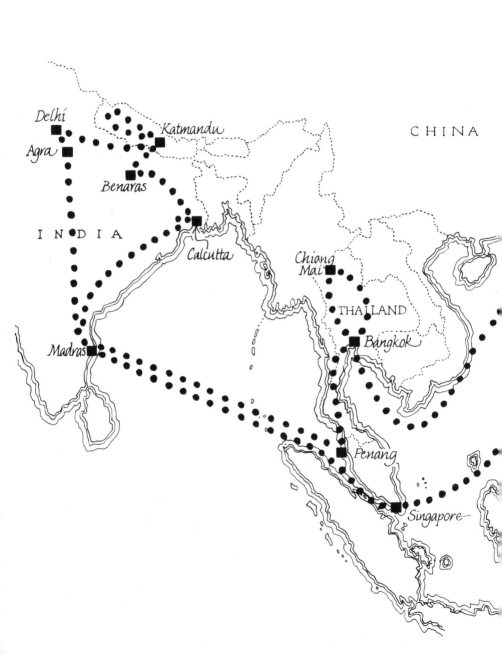

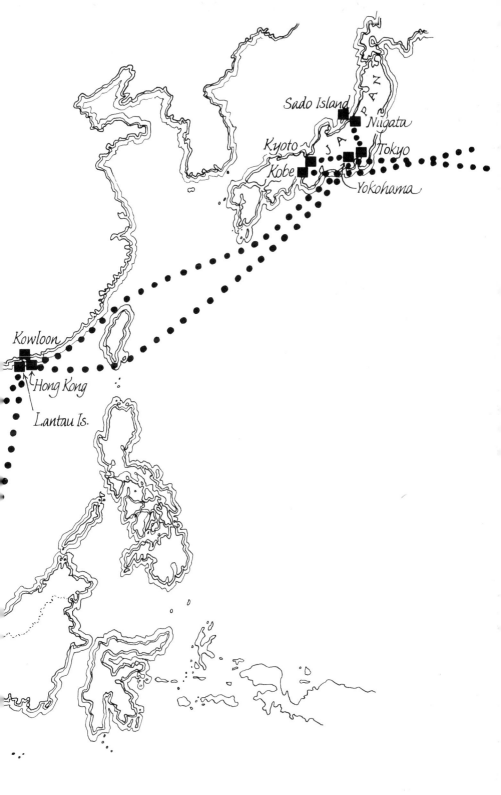

RETURN TO SENDER

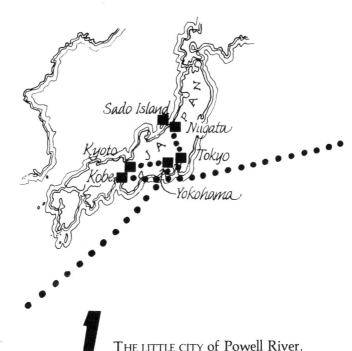

1 THE LITTLE CITY of Powell River, British Columbia, lives on logs cut from the spectacular forests of western Canada, processed and sliced, ground and pummeled to newsprint paper through the huge turbines of the MacMillan-Bloedel Company mill. Fresh and raw as the first cut in an old maple tree, the land on which the town rests appears from the air as a clearing in wilderness. Black smoke darkens the sky over Powell River's Pacific sunsets. When the work is good and overtime plentiful, the Rodmay Pub across from the mill is recklessly full of men and smoke and endless talk.

Ships of all nations, but especially Russian tankers and Japanese containerized-cargo vessels, call at Powell River for

3

wood — for whole trees, cut logs, all the great but limited energy of the earth surface — to be sailed across the wide water to Japan. Japan can use all the good lumber Powell River can deliver. Japan is footing the bill and razing the mountains. The Rodmay is open twenty-four hours.

It doesn't take much of a background in economics to wonder at the impossible ingenuity of Japan. Logging has ceased to provide much of a living in North America itself; the idea that whole trees could be worth shipping five thousand miles across the sea, then returned to us at a profit to the sender, is perplexing to the very men who are downing the timber.

My first awareness of Japan came in the early 1950s when I was growing up in Massachusetts. It was not an awareness of a military enemy, since I was born after World War II and Japan and America seemed to resolve their differences swiftly and amicably; it was a time when GIs were bringing home Japanese wives. I first saw "Japan" stamped on the bottom of a plastic toy I bought in a candy store and cherished in my little boy's pocket. "Made in Japan." I asked my mother where it was.

She replied that it was a faraway place where the people liked us. But they didn't like us during the war. That we owned Japan now. And that things made there broke easily.

Things made there *did* break. They had a delicate — some would say flimsy — quality which collapsed under the rough handling of the typical American child. But if you could master a certain light touch, your Japanese bicycle or yo-yo might last as long as its American-made counterpart and, because they were so much cheaper, I and most kids ended

4

up with hundreds of Japanese playthings in the course of our childhood. To me, Japan was the source of marvelous paper fishes, brightly colored mobiles, and plastic soldiers two inches high.

In high school I read the stories and saw the movies about Japan's role in World War II; particularly memorable was the motion picture version of the Bataan Death March, which portrayed sadistic Japanese officers inflicting horrible torments on their American prisoners. (And they did.) But I never saw a movie about the Japanese-American prisoners in California detainment camps, nor about the atomic bombing of Hiroshima and Nagasaki. These bombings were of course equally horrible and set the precedent for what later became the uniquely American style of tormenting Asian people with fire dropped from the air. Millions of tons of fire fell on Vietnam in the two decades to follow.

In August 1965, in observance of the twentieth anniversary of the atomic nightmares at Hiroshima and Nagasaki, I destroyed my draft card with several hundred other young Americans. I was nineteen, idealistic, completely opposed to our presence in Vietnam, and willing to sacrifice my college career and civic standing if necessary — willing, maybe even anxious, to go to jail in protest of the killing.

In the meantime, Japan, which had so thoroughly accepted defeat and occupation at the end of the war and had embraced American business and manufacturing techniques and even American dress, was turning out higher-and higher-quality goods every year in greater and greater quantities. Radios, televisions, watches, and electronic equipment from Japan came to be the best in the world. And, ironically,

Japan was *not* officially complaining to the U.S. about its actions in Vietnam. Tied as she was to the U.S. economy, it would have been inexpedient for her to break with us on the issue of Vietnam; yet it was hard to believe that any Asian people could condone the American military's massive attempt to subjugate Vietnam. And in fact the young people in Japan, like young people everywhere, were demonstrating their disapproval on the streets and in the universities. But the Japanese establishment seemed to willfully ally itself with a white race across the Pacific against another Oriental race only a two-hour flight away. People in other Asian countries came to resent Japan's economic stranglehold on them too.

In striving to be so much like the Americans in these years, Japan gradually lost interest in her own traditional ways of being — established religion such as Zen Buddhism and Shintoism lost ground rapidly, and traditional music, dance, and theater were eclipsed by imported popular music from the United States and Japanese versions of Western-style entertainment. Some of the energy of the ancient Japanese spirit moved across the water to the West Coast of the U.S., until Suzuki Roshi, the greatest of the Zen masters, found himself living in San Francisco in 1971. Gary Snyder, Jack Kerouac, and others of the Beat generation of writers embraced Zen and popularized it among a following generation of hip readers. Chopsticks and tempura appeared on fashionable American tables at the same time that knives, forks, and spoons — and steaks — were being introduced in Japan.

I first came under the spell of Japan in the mid 1960s, and it was a definitely spiritual attraction. At the time, I was

6

searching, as young men will, for the secret of the universe. Sitting still cross-legged in the Zen position, doing absolutely nothing and thinking absolutely nothing, helped me clear my mind for some powerful awarenesses. Naturally this Zen consciousness, so silent and private, has never been spelled out in words. I ate raw fish too, and listened to plunking koto music on records. Two of my most loved friends joined Zen monasteries in the late sixties and haven't come back.

But merely sitting still didn't satisfy me as I hoped it would. Kerouac said it all in one line: "I am the Buddha known as the Quitter." I was also aware of Japan as a super-power on the material plane, and wondered what irresistible energy could have made the people of this tiny nation such patient Zen sitters, fierce warriors, and now incredibly productive workers. Japan, though small and lacking natural resources, had consistently proven herself a formidable world power since she was first opened to foreign influence and visitors a scant hundred years ago. I wondered about her secret.

There was one other aspect of Japan which really aroused my curiosity and finally bagged me. She seemed doomed to lose. Hundreds of years of extreme efforts to keep Japan closed to the West were abandoned when Commodore Perry threatened to open fire on Tokyo Bay from his gunboats. World War II was a fatal mistake, a gross miscalculation, if you will, of Japan's capacity to fight, a telling disgrace to the honor and infallibility of the emperor. Even the "economic war" of the yen versus the dollar was bound to backfire. A mystic in Nepal once advised me that Japan bears the astrological sign of Pisces — looked at on the map, Japan actually resembles a fish — and with the sign come all the Piscean qualities of self-sacrifice and renewal of life through death. Pisces is the end. "New ideas are born in the West now," my friend Kenji said to me, "and they come to Japan to die." Defeat and setback do not seem to alter Japanese enthusiasm for work. The people simply rebuild what falls down. They retrieve their loss. They start over.

The Japanese lose, and they lose gracefully. They insist on it. And they insist that it be spectacular. That is their special way to gain grace. In reference to World War II, Japanese people, and especially older ones, will sometimes say, "There is no way to apologize." Their natural resources are few and their cities polluted and crowded almost beyond redemption. But Japanese are graceful, talented, imaginative, and, in person, extremely kind and loving in their fashion.

My decision to make the journey came at a moment when I had both the time and the company to do it. I was living alone in San Francisco, sleeping in my friends' apartments and writing a book on the run. For a time I lived in the back of a pickup truck with a redwood cabin built on it; I'd park it on level streets in the Mission District and use a friend's place for toilet and bathing facilities. I was not tied down to any project or place or people but was a wandering, actually homeless person — still no hobo, since my circumstances were comfortable enough, but completely open to suggestion. When I found Paul Williams, a writer and music critic and an old friend, as eager to travel as I was, we began plotting how to get the necessary money; since the spirit to leave was irresistible, the money finally presented itself, following a lot of hard work. We drove from San Francisco to Seattle at

Christmas time in 1971, and from there up to British Columbia, where we sailed from Vancouver. In these final weeks of traveling up the Pacific coast, I finished my book and both of us more or less concluded our affairs in North America. We paid our debts and found new lovers and left feeling no necessity to return if we didn't choose to.

The captain and crew of the American containerized-cargo vessel *Japan Mail*, registered in Seattle, apparently found us odd characters. They had feelings about "hippies" and the like which had gradually disappeared among more sophisticated circles of people. They were themselves strictly crewcuts who liked war movies on Wednesday nights and meat and potatoes three times a day, and their rooms were decorated to resemble a chain motel. There were only two other passengers (the ship could carry a maximum of ten), the more conventional married couple in middle years taking a vacation. They were bound for Australia ultimately, to examine the possibility of living there. They believed America to be in deep trouble, and now that the kids were grown up . . . . The ship's officers and the other passengers remained distantly polite to us, of course, since there is no call for ill feeling out to sea; but we felt more isolated and trapped during that ten-day crossing than either of us ever before had. I read *Autobiography of a Yogi* by Yogananda and sat cross-legged in the closet of our stateroom. We had a generous lump of hash which we smoked until it failed to produce any effect, and many books to read which we never got to. We slept a great deal of the time and ate far too much for our bodies to digest with so little exercise. The only place to walk outdoors was a narrow deck which ran the length of one side of the ship; but the weather was too cold and stormy to invite more than a two-minute stroll twice a day. The ship's library was full of Reader's Digest Condensed Books. The view from our window was of the wild sea surrounding a deck full of boxcar-sized aluminum containers. On this particular voyage, most of the containers were empty — to be filled in Japan with merchandise — because the U.S. West Coast dock strike had made it impossible to load them. The ship was thus light and rode high in the water, which made it toss and roll more forcefully.

Anticipation of what was to follow in Japan was of course the theme of this long daydream. That the anticipation bore no relation to the reality scarcely mattered later. Time passed.

Several days before we landed at Kobe, I had the strange inclination, bolstered by Paul's encouragement, to cut off my hair — which I did, to a scalp-hugging length. Even more unconventional, I agreed to abandon the hashish by giving it to one of the crew members before going through Japanese customs. Thus I entered Japan feeling naked. The ship's officers also found my new hair, or lack of it, curious and maybe even suspicious.

When the day of our arrival dawned, Kobe was already visible on the horizon as the sun rose. Smaller ships and fishing vessels were all around us and the land in the distance smoking up the sky. It seemed to take interminable hours for the ship to approach the city port. As it grew closer, forms of highways and factories began to take shape and the majestic snow-capped Mount Maya loomed up behind all. Cranes and scoops of all kinds were digging busily at the mountain — trying to clear it away, in fact, to make more room for the city's expansion. Even from a quarter mile out to sea, Kobe looked frantic. But the long indisposition of the ocean voyage had left us eager for land and action. The pilot ship came out to guide us into port and a cordon of smartly dressed slim Japanese officers marched up the stairs to our deck; none said a word but one searched my eyes. A polite customs official in a business suit welcomed us in a formal but genial way, and offered his card should we get lost or need his help in any way once in Kobe.

Minutes off the ship, we were pitched into an enormously exotic and confused downtown situation with taxis and crowds, department stores, subways, pedestrian overpasses, and huge neon signs. Kobe is relatively small and simply laid out, though, and we were able to find the local YMCA after getting lost only once. I asked a store clerk for directions to a street — pronouncing the name of the street as instructed on a tourist map — and was astonished when she left her cash register and led us by the arm up the avenue to the right intersection, bowed and smiled, and ran off.

At the same time, something awesome and frightening was going on inside my heart. I felt, for no clear reason, that if I did not escape from Japan that day, if I allowed myself to sleep in Japan even one night, that I would be bound to stay for a very long time and possibly the rest of my life. The place was just that attractive in a demonic way. I could not confess this paranoid and perhaps insane reaction to anyone and waited in the YMCA hotel room until late that night, when Paul had already fallen asleep. Then I gathered up my things and left the room, intending to flag down a cab and go to the nearest airport to wait, awake, for the next flight to

Hong Kong. With a great knapsack strapped to my back, I tiptoed down the stairs, actually fearing the terribly polite desk clerk might be so wounded by my desire to leave that she'd prevent me from getting out. However, I was relieved to find the front desk unoccupied when I reached the lobby.

I made for the big glass doors to the street but stopped cold and shivering in my tracks ten feet away. They were locked from the inside. They were bound together by a huge heavy chain joined by an enormous padlock. Nobody saw me weeping on the polished linoleum floor of the lobby.

2 A KIND OF self-preservation instinct gradually overcame my sorrow, and I began puzzling how to escape the hotel. Since the front door was so firmly padlocked, I investigated the windows and found I could open them — but the drop to the street was long, the earth below paved with concrete and broken glass, and a high wrought-iron fence surrounding the lot looked hazardous to say the least. Moreover, I knew I'd be spotted escaping out the front windows in full view of the street and didn't want to risk being arrested as a burglar. I burrowed down into the basement and found a back door, also locked, which opened into a quiet courtyard surrounded by the same high fence but not facing any traffic. The back door was my last hope.

It had a spring lock, the kind that any experienced person can pick with a popsicle stick, which is exactly what I did, having found one on the floor. I walked out, leaving the door wide open just for spite, and scaled the high fence with some difficulty. That left me on the street past midnight with no place to go and not the faintest idea how to express myself to barkeepers and taxi drivers. I started walking toward the train station.

Kobe at that hour of night was anything but quiet; in fact, she roared. Dazzling rows of headlights on rushing cars, splashy neon displays, stumbling drunks lurching around the pavements, painted women winking at me all left me feeling like a little lost boy in some dangerous downtown neighborhood.

My sense of danger was not mistaken, but it was not the same danger one feels in similarly large cities of the West. I didn't know it at the time, but street crimes such as mugging, robbery, and rape are extremely uncommon in Japan. Even in Tokyo one can walk unmolested by fellow human beings at any hour, any place. But the real dangers are environmental and mechanical — the cars, bridges, trains, and buildings all feel perilously insubstantial — and spiritual/sexual; one gets the feeling that the people will eat you up, body and soul. Some perverse and repressed instinct in me wanted desperately to be devoured, but faced with the actual prospect I panicked. There is an idea in the West that Japanese sexual relations are colored by violence and sadomasochism and enjoy at least the *simulation* of rape; and though the idea is just another stereotype, I found my intuition to be the same.

14

The train station was dark and I kept walking. The fifty-pound weight of the knapsack on my back began to eat into my shoulders. I was dimly aware of being hungry but unable to find a simple restaurant. The drinking establishments all served food but were unapproachable.

Meanwhile, back at the YMCA, Paul Williams was sleeping unaware and a third guy, one of the crew members of the *Japan Mail*, was attempting to get into our room, which we'd rented as a trio. He found the front door padlocked of course but managed to get in through the back door I'd left open. Then he taped a message to me onto the front door glass: "Ray, use back door. David." I saw the message still taped there two days later.

I ran out of strength around four or five A.M., fortunately right in front of a tiny hotel built on three or four levels, clean and simple but strange and futuristic. Since the neon sign was still burning (*kangi* characters and the English word "hotel"), I rapped on the door of this little *ryokan* and woke up the mistress. *Ryokan*, or Japanese inns, are invariably managed by women in their middle to late years. The barefoot hostess in a flower-print robe (*yukata*) established the price of a room and asked me in. I entered without removing my brown suede shoes, which caused the poor woman enormous pain and alarm. They were beat-up shoes my mother had bought me a year earlier in Massachusetts — shoes in which I had traveled half the world — big, muddy, messy shoes, not like the polished black lace-up shoes most Japanese men wear. They did a rough job on the soft tatami (rice straw) floor matting, never meant for shoes; but worse than that, I did not understand at all the old woman's

15

agitated pointing at my feet. I imagined she did not like them because they were dirty — that she wanted me to give her my shoes so she could throw them into the garbage! She knelt at my feet and tried to *pull* them off; I resisted with all my might. I imagined myself fighting this urban congestion shoeless, and freaked. It took a good two or three minutes of this tug of war over the shoes before I suddenly came to my senses. And surrendered.

So I was a barefoot prisoner in a strange land where the hotel maids walk into your suite without knocking. And scrub your back in the tub without asking. In fact, the woman *drew* my bath without asking, then ordered me into it, pointing at it and saying, "Bath!" again and again. Having acknowledged defeat over the shoes, I surrendered totally to all the demands this kindly innkeeper made; and having surrendered to her and having slept peacefully under thick silk quilts, I had surrendered to Japan, sought comfort, and abandoned my foolish notions of escape. My room had a midget refrigerator full of cold beer and cheese and meat snacks. The bed was a sailor's dream of perfect love. The bath was scalding and the back rub delightfully relaxing. I drank just enough to get into a mild, pleasant stupor and finally became immobile, happy, private, and satisfied. An inexplicable warmth rose in me. I felt I could begin life again, alone, in Japan.

Up to that time I had been relying on Paul for a good deal of emotional support, but we had been quarreling bitterly since the day we got on the boat together, and by our first night in Japan we definitely wanted to get away from each other. But we were "married," as Paul once said, and found

16

that social pressure and actual concern for protocol forced us, in a crazy way, to remain together; and, like any married couple, we fought in private and presented to our Japanese hosts an image of partnership and togetherness. We were, as well, the only other Americans either of us knew in Japan. Paul was the only other person with whom I could talk, could compare notes at the end of an exhausting day, could share private jokes. And finally, we had a common purse, and in view of the expense of living there, found we needed each other for economic survival. But our relationship was not kind enough in the end to offer much emotional security. Both of us felt alone a great deal of the time. Paul ultimately met and married a Japanese woman, whom he took with him back to the States; meanwhile, I went to India alone to find out the secret.

I can only ask you to put yourself in my shoes, though that may seem impossible. Surely there is some universal human understanding of the motherless child, the homeless adult. Couldn't any of us, after all, up and leave responsibilities behind and wander the face of the planet? All we need is some bitterness behind us, hope before us, and cash on hand. A high tolerance for discomfort helps a lot, but even incompetent sloths can travel now. Moving can be as habitual as any drug.

Hard times slow people down, although out-and-out depressions can make life so unstable that the hobo's road looks more promising than settling in jobless towns. But real travelers don't seem to be dissuaded by mere lack of material resources. In 1972, you could go into Japan with twenty dollars in total resources, as a friend of mine did, and

days spent consuming ruinous amounts of tobacco, alcohol, money, merchandise — why not having fantastic little paper books that open from either end, a pen, a block of black ink in cake form, a warm cotton *yukata* with blue fishes on it to lounge around in your bedding, then a fine Seiko watch, a Sony color TV, why not a Toyota sports car, why not a video-tape unit! A mind expansion of unbelievable proportions, a new way of thinking. A public bath, tiled and hot, with a big mural of mermaids in their forest lagoon. A little baby's ribbon. A new life.

3 WE DISEMBARKED from the bullet-train at its final stop, Tokyo Central Station; I noted the time, 18:22:00, on the digital clocks prominently hung overhead. The train had arrived precisely on schedule. The once impeccable luxury coach was now ankle-deep in paper, cardboard, and glass bottle wastes tossed on the floors by the drunken, partying passengers. We thought we'd somehow gotten onto a car full of people celebrating somebody's birthday or anniversary, but later learned that the Japanese use any long train ride as an excuse for uproarious festivities; and while no Japanese would so much as leave a cigarette butt in an ashtray on the dining table at home, all of them use the trains, streets, sidewalks, beaches, buses, and other public

21

places for disposing of their garbage. It seemed to me it must be an enormous release of tension for them to leave their spotless homes and offices, where nothing is permitted to be even *misplaced*, and throw trash around with hysterical abandon. Special cleaning men are employed to restore each train to its original cleanliness in the five minutes or so in which it waits in the station; then the mountains of debris are hauled off unceremoniously and dumped God knows where. *Newsweek* at this time reported that 55 per cent of the human waste of Tokyo was still being piped directly into Tokyo Bay, untreated.

It took us at least a half-hour just to wind our way out of the area of the tracks and into the huge, high-ceilinged station waiting room. Tokyo Central Station is the nerve center of dozens of different train lines — subways underground, city-wide surface trains, suburban elevated lines overhead, and special tracks for the superexpress trains. There's an east exit and a west exit which deposit you on opposite sides of the complex, and if you should end up in the wrong place, you're forced to buy another train ticket for the right to pass through to the other side. There are no sidewalks, tunnels, or bridges crossing the station, which seems an extraordinary architectural oversight until you realize that Japanese engineers, unlike their Western counterparts, simply don't believe in a straight line between two points. It is more interesting, more mysterious, and more Japanese to fashion mazes of narrow, twisting passageways.

The main hall of the station was as crowded as two or three Penn Stations at rush hour; our impression was of thousands of tiny people running intently on their errands,

22

knocking each other to the ground in their anxiety, careening and expanding in every direction as far as the eye could see. I thought of the mad playing cards in the Red Queen's croquet game, and of the old Japanese monster movies on TV which always featured a scene in which mobs of hysterical people are fleeing the creature from the bottom of the sea. We set down our heavy luggage and waited in line at the information desk to get the phone number for the Tokyo YMCA, then waited in line for use of the phone itself. The male voice answering *mushi-mushi* on the other end of the line was barely audible over the clamor in the station. With one finger pressed into my ear as forcefully as I could manage, I explained in slow, simple English that we needed directions to the Y. "Tell taxi," the man said, "tell taxi YMCA — Kanda." And hung up.

We hadn't counted on using the Tokyo taxis, but they proved essential in many situations. In fact, if you can't afford to take them, you're better off not going into Tokyo very much, because until you've acquired enough hard experience to know from memory which train goes where, there will be moments almost every day when *only* a taxi can rescue you from being *hopelessly* lost. With the exception of a few major boulevards, Tokyo streets do not have names, and the buildings and houses on those streets do not have consecutive numbers. A house is numbered by the date on which it was constructed, not by its location — so number 23-112 Soto Kanda may be next door to number 87-347 Soto Kanda, and the Soto Kanda part refers to a general district, not a street. Thus, it is impossible to find anything without being led there first by a friend or guide, then memorizing the

23

walking directions from an established subway stop or landmark, most of which are not so well established that they couldn't disappear overnight. Japanese construction crews work on Tokyo streets in the middle of the night, when the traffic is least intense, and more than once I returned to a favorite restaurant to find it had turned into a boutique, or set out to stroll down a familiar street and found it had vanished.

Taxi drivers take some of the confusion out of it. Being universally honest, eager to help, and ruthlessly speedy, they will eventually get you where you want to go — for the price. You give them as many clues as you can and they puzzle it out. You tell them the family name of the people you want to visit, for example, and they will stop and ask policemen and passersby in the neighborhood, "Do you know Mr. Suzuki Bunji?" They may have to ask scores of people in this world's largest city, but they *always* get their man eventually. Can you imagine a New York cabbie pulling up to the curb on Forty-Second Street and asking everyone if they know a John Polanski who lives around there? Even if you have the exact address of your destination, it won't tell the driver more than the general vicinity. Because of this, most Japanese business and social contacts are made for the first time in a well-known coffee shop or bar, and the foreigner in Tokyo collects a small mountain of scraps of paper, jammed in pockets, detailing arrangements to meet so-and-so at three P.M. in such-and-such a place. If you get lost for an hour, don't fear; your host will wait patiently and apologize profusely when you finally do arrive.

It was dark and raining when the cab delivered us to the Y. The cavernous lobby, furnished with overstuffed armchairs and glass display cases, exuded all the gloom of a Western-style funeral parlor. The rooms cost us four thousand yen a day plus tax, or about fifteen dollars, and were equipped only with narrow cots and small wooden desks. Ventilation and lighting were poor and the noise from the street slowly filled me with rage. The prospect of that hotel as our home-so-far-away-from-home was grim, and at that it was the cheapest hotel we could find and so booked up that the desk clerk couldn't promise us the right to stay more than a few days. We decided to get some dinner in a restaurant, maybe a drink, anything to get out of the Y and into a more cheerful environment.

But the Kanda district is better known for retail outlets and bookstores than for night life, and although we walked for blocks on end in the black downpour, we couldn't locate a single place to eat. Narrow street led into narrow lane and we got more lost every moment. We quarreled incessantly. I felt alone, unloved, lost, cold, and wet. Finally a tiny basement room threw a maize-colored light out onto the pavement, and we peered in the windows to find a miniature restaurant crammed with well-dressed businessmen sitting on stools around a counter. We entered.

There was no place to sit, but a very drunken man in coat and tie made us take his seats; stunned by this courtesy, we thanked him, bowing, and began trying to puzzle out how to order food we couldn't name in a language we couldn't speak. The drunk, unfortunately, wouldn't leave us alone and kept asking lengthy questions we didn't understand and laughing uproariously. "Sukiyaki, sukiyaki!" he shouted, and sukiyaki we got — the most expensive thing on the menu, it cost us more than the hotel rooms. Most Japanese have had no direct experience with Americans, and their preconceived notion is that we are wealthy and *must* be given the best. Shopkeepers are sometimes too embarrassed to sell their lower-quality goods to a white foreigner; friends are often excessively apologetic about the size and comfort of their homes; well-intentioned hosts will go to extreme lengths to spare the foreign visitor any real or imagined discomforts; and until you can articulate your desires in reasonable Japanese, you will automatically be directed to the quality goods, the first-class train car, the best seats in the theater. There was no way I could explain that I was accustomed to sleeping in a sleeping bag and eating brown rice and vegetables.

The following day we began to work on a short list of Tokyo contacts we had acquired before leaving the U.S. — names and addresses of several people who were friends of, or at least had corresponded with, my friends in America. Like any seasoned traveler, I didn't permit myself to *expect* much to come out of these references; many nights in new blue towns had taught me that one can often find more help and kindness from strangers than from friends of one's friends. But the Tokyo phone directory, like the streets, does not list people "alphabetically" — in fact, the Japanese language does not have an alphabet as we think of it, and several days passed before we were able to reach the first contact by phone.

Cathy, one of the women who'd lived in our commune in New England, came from a prominent family in the state of Washington, and her parents had some years earlier given a

26

room in their home to a young Japanese student who spent a year at the University of Washington in Seattle. This student's family in Japan expressed their overwhelming gratitude to their son's American hosts, and had often invited them to visit Japan. "Call Mrs. Nagamine when you get to Tokyo," Cathy told me in drenched Seattle December, "and I'm sure she'll be glad to help you out." Mrs. Nagamine proved to be a woman of some social standing, and her husband was vice president of Kyodo News Agency, the largest news service in Japan and equivalent to UPI or AP. Mrs. Nagamine was evidently surprised to hear from a friend of Cathy's family, but she lost no time in determining our whereabouts and appeared at the YMCA with her younger son Shigeki in less than an hour. They came in a silver Mercedes.

I had never before felt the need to be quite so polite. They inquired why we had come to Japan, and our answers were vague and general — to understand the culture, etc. Mrs. Nagamine was a tiny but heavyset woman, dressed in a simple cloth coat, heavy black nylon stockings for the cold, and what used to be called sensible shoes. Shigeki was clean-cut, dressed in a collegiate fashion of the early sixties, and rather more quiet than his mother. All of us spent a lot of time staring at our feet, and the conversation was hushed and simple. They asked what we needed. We replied, a house to live in. They furrowed their brows and fell into a moment's contemplative silence. A house is one of the hardest things to find in Japan. "You want American-style house?" Shigeki ventured. "No," I replied emphatically, "Japanese house." "*Japanese* house?" Mrs. Nagamine seemed amazed. They promised to find us one after warning that Japanese houses were very small and not well heated, then took us out in the car for a grand tour of the city — impossible to see in the rain and darkness — and a fine meal with beer and sake. They returned us to the Y quite late that evening, promised to keep in touch, and in fact called on the phone every day thereafter to keep track of our activities and report their progress on the housesearching. Shigeki took me aside with a light hand on my shoulder before we parted; staring into my eyes with his own soft brown eyes he said, "Please not to worry; my mother *knows many things.*"

It was Shigeki, too, who first made me aware that the rumblings I'd been feeling were earthquakes one and all. We were tooling around in his little Honda sedan when he pointed to an overhead bridge on which pedestrians were crossing the street and said, "When earthquake comes, bridge falls down. I don't like because traffic cannot go." Earthquake comes! Bridge falls down!

My first taste of Japanese hospitality left me floored — and relieved when it was over. The Nagamines continued to pour enormous favors upon us — introductions, meals, tours, etc., etc.; they bent over backwards for us; and as favor piled on favor, our debt to them grew and grew, and with it the embarrassment of owing so much to a family we scarcely could say we knew. Finally, I presented them with a bottle of expensive Scotch whiskey — thinking to myself what a small token of gratitude it was — and was astounded when they passionately refused to accept it. "It is too great a gift — not necessary," the Nagamines said.

Shopkeepers, train conductors, waitresses, hotel clerks,

and strangers in general were usually very friendly in a businesslike way. It was not unusual for a shop clerk to abandon his or her post and lead us by the hand to our destination — even if it was a competing shop. People were obviously interested in us but would turn away blushing if we caught their eyes and would not themselves initiate a conversation. Most could not speak English, of course, but it wasn't until much later that I realized many people who *did* know some English refused to use it for sheer embarrassment at making some errors in their grammar or vocabulary. (How different from the Thais, who will hustle you mercilessly in their broken English and seem incapable of embarrassment over *anything*.) My private contacts with and through the Nagamine family were, if anything, more formal and polite. We met Mrs. Nagamine and her son many times, for example, before we first met her husband — and through him received special privileges at the private library used by the staff of the American Embassy. Lunches were always more or less dignified affairs, even in their home, at which we asked and answered scores of probing questions. The matter of politics came up only once — theirs were establishment and ours radical, and the topic was abruptly dropped.

Armed with English-Japanese dictionaries, guidebooks, and maps, we went out daily to brave the Tokyo transit system and discover the better-known sights of the city — the flaming Ginza strip, brighter than Times Square — the outrageous port-side bars where painted women cooed at passing sailors over drinks — the famous temples and shrines — grand, glittering department stores — and noted restaurants. But I had to agree with what so many American visitors of the past had said: that it seemed impossible for a foreigner to get really *close* to a Japanese person; and I suspected the reason for that, aside from the formidable protocol, was that to be really close meant you could never escape! Such a friendship, a Japanese friendship, would endure throughout your life if it got started at all; and a Japanese love affair! It was frightening! A Japanese love affair might cost your life. People in Hollywood may call each other darling at the drop of a hat, but their insincerity is as notorious as their business dealings are untrustworthy; people in New York, Paris, and London know how to put each other off with flawless politeness, and even marriage is no serious commitment anymore. But if someone in Tokyo makes you a deal, you can be sure he means it, and if someone says, "I love you," you can be sure you're sunk! One of the first and most common English phrases a Japanese person learns is "You can be sure," a refreshing and terrifying consolation in an age where nothing is certain.

Another phrase you'll hear often is "I (he, you) better do it." "You better go see the Zen priest," Mrs. Nagamine would say; and while she meant only that it would be good if I did, it's impossible for an American to overlook the *clearly threatening* overtones of the phrase "you better." I had been told I'd better do this and that hundreds of times before this paranoia began to wear off.

And the truth is, Japan and America are fast friends and lovers. Each looks to the other for inspiration and the young people in either place dream of being each other's magnetic counterparts. Since World War II, Japan has actually been married to the United States; she has played the role of wife;

30

she has had the yen while we have had the buck. That marriage turned old and sour, and as with most modern couples, the wife began to exert her real power over the husband — the yen proved stronger than the buck could have imagined. Underlying the friendship there is some envy, and underlying the love some deadly hatred; that too is a normal matrimonial state. To feel that intense love and sexual attraction for Japan and the Japanese, as I did, and that intense hatred at the same moment drove me to fits — quite literally. And those fits somehow coincided with the worst earthquakes, of which Tokyo has hundreds in a year.

Our second week in Tokyo was made electric by the unmistakable beginnings of just such friendship and love. I received a letter from a friend, enclosing the names of two people who had written her a fan letter from Tokyo. Clutching at any open door, I contacted them immediately. They were a married couple about thirty years old; he, Kenichi, had been ousted from Tokyo University (Japan's most prestigious) for radical political activities; she, Elaine, had been born in New York, met her husband in Chicago, and was realizing her dream of becoming Japanese through him, his family, and her own studies. Kenichi's great-grandfather was easily the most famous samurai warrior of nineteenth-century Japan; the mere mention of this ancestor's name would send any Japanese person into revery. Together they had abandoned worldly, academic, and political ambitions and were studying martial arts — swords! beautiful and threatening swords! — with an eighty-year-old master. Both spoke so softly we had to lean forward to catch their words. They came to the YMCA Hotel for us

31

too, toured us through the university district, took us to a good *cheap* restaurant, shared our political reality, and also liked to smoke marijuana and walk around the streets. Kenichi believed the end of the world was due — and in Tokyo it's hard to believe otherwise; but he was the first to have the courage to say so. Somehow we'd found the heart of a dissident, unsatisfied young Japan in the body of the oldest, noblest families. We were ecstatic.

By this time I realized we really needed a full-time guide — someone of our own age, sharing our interests, who could open the doors to the private worlds and circles of friends of our generation. Miraculously, that person appeared at the YMCA on my twenty-sixth birthday. Any American who stays in Japan, if he or she has enough perseverance, will find just such a guide — a sailor would meet other sailors, a businessman other businessmen, and so forth. We met Kenji Muroya, twenty-three years old, longhaired, consciously committed to a radical view, passionately devoted to rock music, son of a former Japanese ambassador to the United Nations. He'd spent a year in New York, read dozens of youth-oriented magazines from the States, and translated books about rock from English into Japanese. He was perfect.

Kenji knew both Paul and me by our reputations. He flattered us with unearned compliments and seemed quite astonished and excited by our presence. Just as Japanese businessmen had taken on the trappings of American commerce — down to the suits and ties — their children had taken on Bob Dylan and the Rolling Stones, long hair, dope, and a certain contempt for the establishment. Japanese student militants could be immensely more violent than American ones, just as the Japanese establishment could be more successful and efficient at controlling the society. It's not fair to say they are imitating us, though, because in everything they do they are unique. The trappings of counter-culture became a bit exaggerated in Japan and a few years outdated; Kenji and his friends were eager to discover LSD in 1972, whereas most of my friends, and I myself, had quit using it before 1970. Popular books tended to be published in translation two or three years after their U.S. or European publication, but phonograph records were released simultaneously in Japan, since no transalation effort was required. In fact, you could hear the very latest pop music from the U.S. in thousands of coffee shops all over Japan, even though at least 95 per cent of the audience couldn't understand the words. Neil Young's album *Harvest*, with its hit song "Heart of Gold," followed us everywhere.

"I want to live, I want to give
I been a miner for a heart of gold...

I been to Hollywood, I been to Redwood,
I crossed the ocean for a heart of gold...

I been in my mind, it's such a fine line
Keeps me searchin' for a heart of gold
And I'm gettin' old..."

To celebrate my birthday, I took the train down the coast to Kamakura, an hour and a half from Tokyo and the birthplace of much of Japan's spiritual heritage. Today Kamakura is a seaside resort and her famous temples,

33

shrines, and sixty-foot-tall bronze Buddha are major tourist attractions. The place is fairly crowded by any standard except Tokyo's; in comparison to the city, it seemed pleasantly relaxed. The movie houses and nightclubs were less gaudy and prices on everything less expensive. I sat in the warm February sunshine at the foot of the Buddha most of the afternoon, lost in a dream mixture of my present homesickness and my future family; I had a vision, more powerful than anything I've experienced before or since, an actual vision of a madonna and child. I went to the beach and kicked a can around the half-moon bay, then ate a club sandwich at a seaside restaurant with a spellbinding view of the water. I rode back to Tokyo on the train trembling violently and struggling unsuccessfully to hide it from the other passengers.

Meanwhile, Paul had been telling Kenji that what I needed most for a birthday gift was some marijuana. Grass is incredibly difficult to come by in Japan, virtually impossible for foreigners, since the paranoia level is as high as the penalties are steep; and the price, when you can get it, is never less than fifty dollars an ounce. Japanese police are ruthlessly efficient because law-abiding citizens, once aware of a crime being committed, will voluntarily inform them of it. There is nothing like the widespread American notion that the only crime is getting caught. Nonetheless, I returned to find a mysterious package of gift-wrapped joints — my first and finest gift from the nation of Japan — with a card reading, "I have made this marijuana so American friend can get high." I found this thoughtfulness deeply moving.

I once received a tiny quantity of opium (which made me

34

sick), ran to the dictionary to find the Japanese word for "opium," and found how to say the phrase "There are no opium users in Japan." "Wrong!" Kenji laughed. "There is *one!*"

From the moment Kenji walked in, we were more and more deeply involved in a frantically social life among peers. Two or three days later, the management of the YMCA began incongruously pressuring us to get out of their hotel, and we soon found ourselves on the street with heavy bags and not the faintest idea where to go. We took a taxi to Kenji's apartment and asked to store our luggage there. By the time night fell, there was no alternative but to go to sleep with three or four others on the soft tatami matting on the floor of the Mejiro District apartment. Having done that once, and enjoyed it, there was no reason not to go on doing so until the Nagamines found us a house. We took up eating and sleeping on the floor of the tiny house which Kenji shared with his girl friend Reiko, her sister Yuko, and scores of shaggy friends; spent most of our days like the others in coffee shops, theaters, stores, subways, and libraries and recongregated nightly in the late hours for tea and conversation followed by sleep if one had time for it; and never used a hotel again.

4 FALLING INTO Japanese hospitality is like falling into debt. In the case of our peers, it was comfortable and reassuring; in the case of older sponsors such as the Nagamines, it could be restricting. But in either case, when someone you scarcely know is bending over backwards to help you, "special for you," you feel in their debt, which is precisely the point. They'd rather have you in *their* debt than be in *yours.*

Kenji lived with pretty, soft Reiko in her three-room Mejiro District apartment on the fourth floor of a gray nondescript apartment building hiding in an alley off the main street. Reiko and her younger sister Yoko — twenty-one and eighteen respectively — were the official residents of the flat, which was rented by their mother. Mother lived in Sendai far to the north, but still checked up on her daughters by phone and had her matronly friends in Tokyo call periodically to make sure everything was all right. Neither Kenji nor any other man could answer the telephone in that house, although 90 per cent of the calls were for him. Kenji was at the center of a wide circle of translators, writers, students, musicians, artists, and revolutionaries who called on him at all hours of the night, and more than once the whole crowd had to be secreted out the door just in time for the arrival of one of Mother's spies. A great air of secret salon hung over the tiny Mejiro House. Bedtime was dawn, and fluffy *ftons* were spread over the floor to accommodate however many people cared to sleep. Utter chaos blew through that apartment, but in time it felt like home to me, a perfect Japanese equivalent of various low dives I'd lived in in my student/radical years in Boston, New York, Washington, D.C. The Mejiro House was alternately warm and safe or frightening and maddening.

The living room was small — eight mats — perhaps ten feet by ten feet. The floor was soft and many pillows were scattered about underfoot, where they fought for space with books and records stacked against the walls. The bedding was kept in the closet.

One window of this main room opened onto a tiny balcony with a view of Tokyo roof tops, power lines, and the moon. Many nights I chartered the lunar cycle through that strange window, wondering in my quilts if I was dreaming this whole experience. English writers have been notoriously poor at transmitting the *feeling* of Japan to their readers back

37

home in the West — perhaps because details such as these don't really suggest how exotic and different the Japanese *mind* is. Lafcadio Hearn, a real American hero in Japan, ended up saying, "I feel *something unspeakable* towards Japan." He meant, of course, something beyond his own understanding. Anyway, the Japanese "living room" is for eating, drinking, sleeping, conversing, and dreaming. It's like a delicate cage that sways in the wind, or when the earth shakes, complete and autonomous, it is a Life Box. Millions of them stand in rows.

The adjoining kitchen was taken up mostly by the functional necessities of the household, although there was a small table with three stools, good for sitting down to read, work, chat, or smoke. (Japanese are the world's heaviest cigarette consumers, and I found I needed two packs at least to get through a day in Tokyo.) There was a small refrigerator, two-burner gas stove (just the iron framework and the burners themselves, no casing), sink and garbage can, washing machine, bathroom sink, and mirror. Off the kitchen, a tiny toilet room and, separate from that, a tiny bathroom. (In Japan one would never eliminate body wastes in the same room in which one bathes. The toilet may be littered with newspapers and cigarette butts, especially in a public place, but the bath, even if public, is always impeccably clean.) Off the kitchen was a small entranceway where shoes, umbrellas, and packages were left. Umbrellas, by the way, are so popular that at the slightest sign of rain all the sidewalks of Tokyo seem to be covered by one moving carpet.

Besides these rooms, there was also a bedroom just big

enough for a bunk bed, Western style. Yuko, the shy younger sister, slept in that dark sanctuary. Kenji and I slept there only once in the aftermath of an LSD trip which he'd insisted I provide — it was his first trip and my last.

The insanity which I and others suffered was rooted in our utter lack of privacy in Mejiro House. I felt ashamed, maybe even bourgeois, but I missed having a house with a room in it where I could shut the door, shut out the world. The most privacy I could achieve in Japan was in the midst of a crowd — in a coffee shop, at a temple, on a long train ride. Only twice did I go to a *ryokan* and rent a private room, but even such expensive accommodations become private only beyond the hour at which the hostess stops walking in on you.

After a month in Mejiro House, Paul and I were stir crazy, to say the least. I used to run out at three A.M. to sit and moon in a cute second-story coffee shop around the corner, which served only hot dogs and spaghetti. Just at the breaking point the impossible happened (again): Mrs. Nagamine found us an executive's summer house by the sea in Chigasaki, an hour's ride south of Tokyo. The new Chigasaki House was a dream come true — a trim suburban ranch-style house by a farmer's field, painted shocking pink with one entire side made of sliding glass doors. The heavily littered beach was a quarter mile from the house, over a golf course, and across from a high-speed expressway. We had a Western living room with couch and armchairs, TV and coffee table; a great kitchen with all the amenities, even including a stock of food; a main sleeping room bigger than I could have imagined because of its lovely emptiness. And the

39

rent was 50,000 yen, $175 a month — unbelievably cheap! The least expensive one-room apartment in Tokyo was $400 a month plus a nonrefundable $2,000 down payment. None of our beloved friends in Tokyo could have rented the Chigasaki House at any price; once again we were lucky victims of a peculiar favoritism which is sometimes showered on foreign visitors.

There was only one hitch. The Chigasaki House was occupied, and would remain occupied for at least another month, by a policeman!

Katsuta-san, who was said to be "the best policeman in all of Kanagawa Prefecture," was our new roommate.

How we were to reconcile our fondness for illegal drugs and our Tokyo friends' late-night habits with Officer Katsuta's workaday schedule and weakness for Scotch whiskey was beyond us and left us a bit worried. But, fortunately for us, Mrs. Nagamine had somehow gotten the idea across to the man that we were distinguished/famous visitors from the U.S., and Katsuta-san was as strenuously polite as the others — a real sweetheart in fact, he went out of his way not to notice what was going on. When he found us blowing joints in the kitchen, he dashed off and came back with a gift bottle of Scotch! When he heard that we liked poetry, he composed a haiku for us, and illustrated it with a picture of the moon; his calligraphy was exquisite. Even armed with dictionaries, we could barely communicate with him, but he took us to his favorite *sushi* restaurant in the nearby town and arranged a carte blanche free feast. When our friends came and made noise, he stayed in his room and pretended not to be disturbed, though the walls were paper. We couldn't have anticipated that the best policeman in all of Kanagawa Prefecture would also be the poet, painter, secret drinker, and charming, sensitive soul that he was.

The woman who lived next door was equally polite but not so easy to please; her relationship to the landlord and the Nagamines was never fully explained to us, but she seemed to be responsible for the house in *some* curious way, and she appeared every now and then to give us the phone or power bills and generally examined things. I remember vividly, and can still feel the pain of embarrassment, that this elderly woman happened to step into the kitchen on a day when I hadn't cleaned the top of the stove since the previous night's spaghetti dinner. The stove was covered with greasy red blotches which she immediately noticed, naturally didn't mention. I spent the whole day in convulsions of shame, not even stopping to realize that having a dirty stove wasn't the worst crime in the world. In the context of a visit from the landlord's appointed caretaker, it was practically the worst thing I could have imagined. Little things assume big proportions where honor and correct conduct are issues, and I felt — certainly for the first time! — mortified by my slovenliness as a guest in someone's home. (For, even as a tenant, one feels a guest.) I scrubbed the whole kitchen clean after she left, but of course my conscience was my only witness. Katsuta returned from work in his Honda sedan to compliment me on my effort, saying that no Japanese *man* could have cleaned the kitchen so well! And I felt a little better.

When Katsuta left to get married, the house quieted down and I used it as my retreat from the madness of the Tokyo social whirl, which Kenji had thrust us into headfirst. Every day, it seemed, we rode the commuter trains into Tokyo, and every night returned to the little house in Chigasaki, where Paul read books and wrote letters and I got drunk — dead drunk.

On the vernal equinox in late March, a group of twelve friends, led by Kenji and Reiko, came to visit us in Chigasaki and slept over with us in our two matted rooms. They were all people whose hospitality I had enjoyed in Tokyo, and I would have been delighted to see any one or two of them in our home. But all together, which is the way most people do everything in Japan, their arrival had the effect of making me feel invaded. My private, peaceful, alcoholic home, heated only by a small electric stove with two horizontal red bars glowing in an equal sign, was suddenly so full of people there wasn't a cubic inch of private space available. I had a classic claustrophobic reaction and went running out the door, heading for the beach.

Outside the pink rancher a wrathful wind was blowing from the ocean. It is called *Haru Ichiban*, the first wind of spring, and it always comes to Japan around vernal equinox time; but I didn't know that at the time. I struggled across the golf course by putting my shoulder into the fierce hurricane-strength gusts, and looked up only once to see a Japanese businessman/golfer (insanely) whacking the ball into the wind with a grand swing. He was alone. Beyond the golf course I crossed the highway, passing the beach-front bowling alley and heading for the water. The beach itself was lost in a whipping sandstorm and washed by an angry sea.

Some unnameable compulsion made me continue walking to the shore, though I was doubled over and protecting my face in my hands against the sand pebbles stinging my skin. When I felt the water touch my toes, I looked up and out — toward California, I thought — and saw instead a boat, bobbing and reeling in the violent waves. It was coming in.

From all appearances it was a sailboat, but no sails were up and there was only a stump where the mast should have been. The closer it came in, the more it looked like a wreck, a victim of the storm. I stood rooted to the spot, pulling it in with my will and heart. When it came within a few feet of shore, I ran and got the neighbors to help, and we hauled it in. Three men out sailing on holiday had died aboard it, trapped in the cabin.

Haru Ichiban, the first wind of spring. Vernal equinox, "no more cold." It seemed to me that I had been selected, somehow, to play messenger of death, death's discoverer, in the rebirth of the year. I went back to the house prepared to apologize to my friends for having so rudely dashed away from them. They sensed what was bothering me and rushed to apologize for "disturbing your work." After many rounds of "So sorry," we all sat down to smoke a joint — fourteen people on one joint — and we all got high. I tried to explain what had happened on the beach in sign language and simple Japanese, and actually reenacted the scene in a kind of impromptu ballet. I spread my arms wide to represent, to be, the wind.

Once settled into our new home, we found we still had to make the trip into Tokyo by Japan National Railroads virtually every day. Kenji had invariably arranged lunch, snacks, dinner, meetings, conferences with magazine editors, publishers, musicians in studios, advertising copywriters on location on the streets. I loved every minute of these high-speed, usually confusing adventures. I was never photographed so often, in so many poses — some obscene, which everyone enjoyed in delightful Japanese lust for the unmentionable. Everyone seemed to have a camera and a watch.

But the trip into town was no pleasure. The commuter trains which snake around Tokyo in every which way are not like the plush Tokaido Line express trains, but more austere, crowded, and dirty. Most of the time we couldn't find a seat and had to stand all the way surrounded by sleeping, upright executives. As far as I could tell, all Japanese can sleep soundly while standing up, even hanging on a subway strap! I wondered whether it came from their being carried on their mothers' backs in a tightly bound, perfectly upright position, as all babies are. On the ride back home at night, particularly if it was late, the trains were full of obnoxious silly drunks. The more you ride the JNR, in fact, the more loathsome it becomes, not only for foreigners but for everyone; and the crowded, inhuman conditions to which the passengers are too often exposed would probably provoke daily riots anywhere other than Japan. The trains in India are worse, to be sure, but *there* the passengers *will* riot at the slightest provocation; Japanese just ride along and suffer silently. When the JNR goes out on strike, which seems to happen several days a year by some polite arrangement between management and labor, the population is struck with real pandemonium and congestion almost beyond tolerance. People who have absolutely no other way to get home sit on railway station floors for forty-eight hours without moving. And most of them without complaining!

44

Even if you can afford one, the hotels are full and the normally choked traffic becomes utterly impossible.

One of the greatest pleasures I've ever felt, however, was getting *off* my train at home in Chigasaki, boarding my little bicycle and peddling home to our house, perhaps stopping enroute for some groceries or postage stamps or liquor in one of the quiet shops along the way. There, you'd always have time for a few pleasant words with the merchant — even if they were the same words you exchanged every day, the only words you knew. And, at home, the bath was waiting and the phone could be taken off the hook. Following a bit of food cooked up in the kitchen, I'd generally start making myself drinks — gin and tonic or bourbon and water or hot sake — and it was a rare evening that I didn't end up totally drunk in a quiet, repressed condition. Most of Japanese television was superviolent blood-and-gore melodrama — not offensive but not interesting — and sober documentaries beyond my comprehension; and since there was little to read in English, I'd often end up staring at the (totally blank) wall for hours while huddled, shivering, in front of the one electric heater which we could afford. And drinking. I never before or since drank with such abandon as in Japan — indeed, it is a national sport. Alcohol, at least if it's made in Japan, is one of the few things that are really cheap. A fifth of the best gin was about $1.80, whiskey about $2.00. A person could drink himself dead at those prices, and I suppose millions have.

Even an astronomical rate of alcoholism doesn't prevent Japanese from working hard, and my own indulgences didn't slow me down either. Most of the business I did with

45

serious publishers, editors, TV producers, or advertising people was accomplished in a public drinking place; as often as not, all parties to the conference were, if not drunk, at least somewhat off balance. The proper host never allows his guest's glass to be empty — literally. After every second or third sip someone would rush forward to refill my glass. Food is the same — the right thing to do is eat until you're stuffed. Meals have no limits, courses keep coming; only after you've refused sincerely and passionately at least three times will they stop producing more magnificent platters — and begin the desserts. In the flush of the 1972 prosperity, with billions of surplus U.S. dollars sitting in Japanese banks and the yen climbing in value every day, all of Tokyo seemed bent on a path of spending *wildly.* I imagined that New York in the 1920s just prior to the Crash might have been similar.

About this time we were running out of the money we'd brought with us from the States and found ourselves faced with the necessity of earning more in Japan if we wanted to stay on. So, in a sense, we were thrown into the job market in Tokyo, and we found it to be a livelier employment prospect than anyplace on earth. In fact, it was difficult *not* to work. There seemed to be no unemployment at all in Japan — also no social security or government pensions for the elderly — and foreigners could teach their own language to the Japanese even if they could do nothing else. English teachers could command about ten dollars an hour as private tutors, but the idea never appealed to us. Instead, Kenji found work for us writing for various hip magazines in town, and I even did some commercial interviews/endorsements for magazine ads for the Hitachi Corporation and wrote advertising copy for the Mitsubishi Corporation. These assignments paid well.

The first article I wrote was a general explanation of how I had come to Japan and why I'd chosen to leave my life in the U.S. Kenji translated it and it appeared shortly thereafter in *New Music Magazine*, which might be compared to our *Rolling Stone*. I remember how proud and delighted I was with the final piece, although of course I couldn't read it. Scores of beautiful young strangers would compliment me on it in crowded rock-music coffee shops, and I felt a warm glow of acceptance.

More articles followed until it seemed I was always working on one piece or another, always had a new one promised to somebody before finishing the last, always had more work to do. I carried around my notebooks and pens like proud tools of my trade. I was a storyteller with an appreciative audience, powerful medicine for a wounded ego, and gratifying enough to make me think seriously of staying on in Japan. Despite the good reception my work had gotten at home, I'd never been so thoroughly flattered there; and even in the context of those odd character-figures running top to bottom on the page, I could recognize the work as my own. All that remained was for me to master the Japanese language so that I could communicate directly and without translation — but I didn't stop to realize that once I succeeded at learning Japanese I'd lose my "special" status of being a newcomer, a cherished and innocent pet. The fact is, although they encourage foreigners to pick up some Japanese language, the Japanese do not really want them to master the tongue, because they can't hide anything from

47

them thereafter. A secretive and clannish race of people, the Japanese are protected by their difficult language, which few foreign visitors ever grasp.

One American who did achieve complete command of Japanese was Jack Stamm, an advertising copywriter and musician who introduced me into his circle of friends and showed me a kind of life that a bright, hip American man could make for himself in Tokyo. From what I could see of it, it was not the life for me; but it *was* better than the sober and self-serving lives of American professors holding forth in Kyoto, surrounded by fawning students and waited on by maids in their impeccable households. Jack was more real than *that* kind of expatriate, and more human than the American businessmen who lived almost totally divorced from all things Japanese except commerce. Jack was a hustler, lived on the streets, free-lanced his living with various companies and agencies, lived by his wits, and talked his way (in Japanese so perfect that cab drivers would spin around in their seats in astonishment) into all hearts and out of all trouble. He never stopped talking, in fact, and spoke at a pace so furious that few could get a word in edgewise.

We met Jack in a famous coffee shop in Roppongi District by the light of the full moon; about forty years old, his long curly hair streaked with gray, he wore a flamboyant pendant over a turtleneck sweater and carried an enormous handbag emblazoned with the symbol for Scorpio, his sun sign. "You guys look like you need to get STONED," he announced, and swept us down the street to a private restaurant on a hilltop where we blew joints under the noses of unsuspecting hostesses, drank heavily, and ate a meal that cost nearly a hundred bucks. From there, into a cab and ZOOM, off to bars and *jamizen* joints all over town, Jack playing instruments, dancing with geishas, more drinking, more smoking, more taxis, until the night was wasted away and I could barely stand up. Jack, the saint adman cosmic prankster, still dancing to the end, flirting with every pretty face, succeeding at hiding his loneliness. Months later he showed me poems he'd written which I thought as beautiful and striking — even peaceful — as any poems I know. But his life was to the contrary — burning up the streets of Tokyo with his unquenchable taste for wine, women, and song. What a sweet, wise, wonderful sad man, this Jack-san.

Jack's business world, the world of advertising, paid the kind of money one needed to support such a Tokyo trip. Since Japan markets her goods to the English-speaking world to such a large extent, English-native copywriters who could also speak Japanese could demand fair compensation for their specialized skills. But the actual work — describing Sony's new autostereo component, for example — was insipid, easy, and uninspiring for Jack's superintellect; I got the idea that he just turned these things out of an evening to get the money to live for a week.

My own experience with the advertising subculture was more pleasant. The men who interviewed me for a series of ads for Hitachi electric razors and stereos were delightful and sincere. Ryo Kusakabe, the chief copywriter for the Nissei Tsushinsa Agency, which handled the Hitachi account, asked me questions about my involvement with the U.S. peace movement and with our communal farm, and more personal questions about my family, childhood, religion, sex life, etc., for an hour or so in a quiet restaurant somewhere on the main Ginza strip. Elfin Ryo, eyes sparkling, was laughing and applauding my replies — our eye contact alone was most of the language we needed. It seemed almost sinful to get paid sixty thousand yen (two hundred dollars) for that hour's "work." Later the interview was wrapped around photos of me and the Hitachi electric razor — a silver bulletlike cylinder that ran on one battery and really did give a comfortable, close shave.

Besides advertising and writing, we took on informal roles as literary agents — bringing new books from American publishers, as often as not written by friends of ours — to the attention of Tokyo publishers. We were not usually paid directly for this referral service, but the gratification of selling a book to a Japanese publisher, bringing that book to the eyes and minds of Japan's readers, was so great that we loved working at it. And the publishers invariably stopped what they were doing and served us tea and snacks.

Our greatest coup was interesting some translators in the Wilhelm edition of the *I Ching*, the ancient Chinese book of changes. Although peaking in popularity in the U.S. in 1972, the *Ching* was still considered an old-fashioned book of interest only to the superstitious elderly in Japan, the ones who patronized yarrowstalk throwers crouched on sidewalks outside major subway stops in Tokyo. The most recent translation of the *I Ching* into Japanese was a difficult two-volume *kangi* translation made at the turn of the century and all but unreadable to modern Japanese, who have adjusted to three major revolutions in their language in the current century. "Old" Japanese is thus painstakingly complicated compared to the "new" *hiragana* phonetic symbols, and young people frequently cannot read anything published before the last war. We managed to get a group of competent people excited about the prospect of translating the Wilhelm edition from English directly into Japanese — by-passing the original Chinese *and* the original German translation. The project would take years, of course, but it was well begun. The *I Ching*, born in neighboring China, will sooner or later make its way to Japan via a round-the-world odyssey in which I was glad to serve as a messenger boy.

But it was the step into television work that finally proved too much for me, and paved my way out of Japan. Word of our being in Chigasaki ultimately reached a producer from NHK-TV, Japan's government-owned network, who came to my house one afternoon with a proposal to make a documentary of my life in Japan for broadcast on his regular series program. The film would show the intermingling of young (read "counter-culture") people from East and West, I'd have some speaking lines, the whole thing would be heavily financed, and would accrue to the reputation and income of friend Kenji as well as myself. It was really irresistible but involved the implicit trap of time: because of conflicting schedules and an already heavy workload, the documentary would consume at least three to six months in the making, and given the vagueness of time considerations in general, might easily take longer. Once committed to it, I could not in good conscience leave it, but I wanted to be on to India sooner than six months off. So I politely declined.

But the NHK executive would not take no for an answer. He called on me at my house, sent his chauffeur-driven limousine to escort me and my friends into Tokyo, wooed me with drinks and food. I liked him enormously and loved being squired around the studios and the whole exciting universe of Japanese electronic media, but I kept insisting that I didn't have the time for his film. (As a compromise, I offered to do it *after* my return from India, but he wouldn't wait that long.) He poured ever more extravagant favors on me in an effort to dissuade me from leaving Japan. Kenji and friends joined this conspiracy until I felt under tremendous pressure. All of them, smiling and laughing, simply refused to believe that I *would* go away, and I could see my path leading to confrontation, disaster, over this issue — the original fear I felt on landing in Kobe rushed back to me in my dreams. Would I be *allowed* to leave?

Finally the NHK man found out about my friend Christine in New York City, the woman who was supposed to have accompanied me to Japan. He offered to place a call to her, get her to come to Tokyo — then I would be less lonely when Paul and Sachiko left to begin their married life in the States. It was clear that if any friend of mine in the States could come and make it possible for me to remain in Japan, the television people would see that it happened. An appointment was made for me to call New York at nine P.M. on a certain weekday night, when it would be eight o'clock the following morning in New York. Again, I declined the favor and said I would not telephone New York, but again Kenji repeated that I should be at the studio at nine, that the phone line would be ready. We were either experiencing a total breakdown in communication, or else Kenji was deliberately ignoring my protests. On the morning of the fated day, sitting in Mejiro House drinking tea, I remarked sadly and without any passion that I wished I were dead. Everybody in the room nodded as if they understood the feeling.

When evening s*ruck, I made a last protest that I wouldn't call New York and went out on the street. At nine P.M. I was standing in front of the Kinokuniya Bookstore in Shibuya Square in Tokyo, realizing that a party of people was waiting for me at the NHK studios, but feeling that it would be futile to communicate with them since they didn't respect my intentions. I went into the bookstore which was still open, and began browsing through the English-language paperbacks in the back stalls.

At 9:10 P.M., the tiny manager of the bookstore came running over to me, smiling and bowing: "You are Raymond-san?" He was carrying a copy of my book *Famous Long Ago* and comparing my face to that on the dust jacket. I admitted my identity and he bowed again: "NHK on the telephone. You are wanted in the studio."

Suddenly a sweeping paranoia came over me. How did they know I would be in this bookstore, when I didn't know it myself? Would "they" also know every place I tried to hide, would the phone ring in every restaurant, apartment, hotel I might flee to? Why did they want me to stay so badly in the first place? And was there anyone among them I could trust — trust, especially, to let me go without this emotional blackmail?

There was one, I thought. I'd met a writer months earlier in the office of a Tokyo rock magazine, a guy who had a keen interest in American outlaws and proudly introduced himself as a Japanese outlaw. He'd given me his secret telephone number, asking me to call if I ever needed a place to hide. So I called and he answered.

"Age, I need a place to hide. They are looking for me everywhere," I said.

"Ah! CIA?" he said.

"No! NHK!" I replied.

Age laughed. "NHK looking for *me* too," he said. We agreed to meet on a busy street corner in twenty minutes. Standing there, I felt his arm lock into mine and he sailed me down the street and into the crowds without saying a word — just winking.

He took me through a maze of back streets to his "pad" — full of the latest American and British rock music albums, even a stick of dynamite grass, even a Western-style bed! Good old Age was as obsessed with my country as I was with his. The phone rang about five minutes after I got there, but he put his finger to his lips as if to say, "We won't answer." And we didn't. The night, or most of it, passed in a dream of Incredible String Band music and grass hallucination. Just before dawn, Age led me to a train line and we parted with hugs.

Back at the Chigasaki House, the phone was ringing constantly, although it was past five A.M. Both Paul and Policeman Katsuta were elsewhere that night, so I had only to let it ring and my caller — undoubtedly, I knew, the NHK studio — would think me absent. I took a hot bath. The phone kept ringing at five-minute intervals. Finally I had to face the music. I picked it up. It was Sachiko, Paul's sweetheart.

"Be careful you," she said. Sachiko was just beginning to

54

use English, and knew only a dozen words. "Be careful you," she said again, and hung up. It sounded like something she'd found in a dictionary as a way to express the concept of DANGER.

The phone rang again. This time it was Reiko, Kenji's girl friend. I thought myself lucky to hear from two such soft and reassuring women in sequence. Reiko's English was much better, and she explained that Kenji and all the NHK people had waited up all night for me at the studio and that all of them were convinced I had committed suicide by throwing myself under a train! I was appalled. It had never occurred to me that they'd wait all night for me; rather I figured they'd understand that I didn't intend to show up and go home. And I couldn't imagine why they'd think I killed myself, since I didn't remember having remarked within Kenji's earshot that I wanted to be dead. (*Wanting* to be dead is of course different from being *willing* to kill yourself, but suicide is so commonplace in Japan that Kenji's premise was not at all far-fetched.)

The next moment was one of the worst in my life. Kenji finally reached me on the phone and devastated my psyche with the heaviest excoriation anybody had ever delivered to me. He said I was selfish, that was the worst. He said I was mean, evil, *and* selfish. That our friendship was finished. That he no longer cared whether I chose to leave Japan. He' said all those kinds of things, and all I could say was "I'm sorry."

The following day Kenji appeared dressed to kill in a business suit with starched dress shirt and tie. I had never seen him in such a get-up. He sat down with me at a restaurant table and began: "Since we are no longer friends, I have only business to do with you so I am dressed for business.''

A few days later all was forgiven, but the sadness lingered on and lingers still — the sadness of knowing that each could be so blind to the other's needs.

In the spring, cherry blossoms
In the summer the cuckoo
In the autumn, the moon
In the winter, the cold, clear, snow.

—YASUNARI KAWABATA
Japan the Beautiful and Myself (Kodansha Ltd.)

5 THE Polish Ocean Lines happened to run a small page-one ad in the *Japan Times* offering a cheap one-week passage to Hong Kong on their freighters just on the day I was ready to sign up. I made a reservation to sail in one month's time. Winter had turned to spring, and I had a month to finish my affair with Japan, but it wasn't enough. Kenji and others continued to object so much to my leaving that I felt free to go only after promising to return to Japan after I left India. That way, no one need say *sayonara* ("farewell"), but only *mata* ("later")! A Japanese friendship is for life, and involves actual responsibilities. To take myself away with no assurance of return would be unfriendly, even cruel, to myself as well as to my friends. The final month in

57

Japan was so packed with action, however, that I left knowing I hadn't been so energized in years, and I was actually anxious to return. Once out to sea, I dreamed of it — fierce, erotic dreams of Japanese eyes filled my sleep.

I searched for the secret behind the Japanese spirit of hard work in the face of overwhelming certainty of disaster. Whatever answers I found were within myself. The hard work definitely served as a distraction from the insane introspection and self-judgment which that society engendered. When loneliness possessed me, I worked harder. When my own worthlessness showed itself too plainly, I buried myself in work. Work and alcohol were the readily available outlets which somehow were not outlawed by polite convention.

The Japanese sincerely believe that suffering is good for you. This is a concept which never made much headway in the West. In the United States, we run in headlong pursuit of our comforts. In Japan, one can still suffer with dignity and get off on it. Martyrdom is the logical conclusion to a life of noble suffering. The masochistic strain finds its perfect complement in an equally sadistic nature. War and sex seem to bring out that sadism. Most Japanese magazines, newspapers and comic books portray sex in both graphic and cruel ways. The standard format shows the man abusing — sometimes bloodily — a submissive, tearful wife.

One's own accomplishments must always be understated; the Japanese language itself is full of honorific forms for addressing others — particularly one's "superiors" — and humbling forms for referring to oneself. Expression of the individual ego is not encouraged, and Japan seems to have produced relatively few outstanding "personalities" in the international sphere, although achieving outstanding power as a nation. Invited to what turned out to be a sumptuous feast, I was led into the dining room of an ex-ambassador's home with the warning "Please come into dinner although there is nothing to eat"! What the hostess meant to convey was that her dinner was really nothing — though it wasn't. Naturally I complimented her on every step of the long and superb meal, and naturally she insisted it was all nothing. "The thing is a no-thing," the words of the Buddha remembered. Many gifts offered came with a built-in apology — "Made in Japan, not so good." Every discomfort, real or imagined, made someone very sorry. I had never seen people apologize to each other so incessantly, and began to see the tremendous pride and superiority-conviction hiding in the cloak of this apparent inferiority complex. He who is last shall be first, and somehow by expecting no recognition a person learns to be happy with any, or none.

The flattering attentions I was getting for my work tended to inhibit my development as a humble and hard-working soul not even expecting the heavenly merit that comes of virtue; but fortunately Japan presented so many obstacles to comfort that my highest flights of egoistic fancy were inevitably followed by the deepest sloughs of despair. Nobody can feel important while riding in a jam-packed commuter train screaming its way through outlying towns near Tokyo. And most people can't feel loved until they feel a sexual vibration coming from the people they are with. In my case the sexual energy was ferocious, unmistakable, earthshaking — I felt it in the bodies of men and women both whom I loved, and who loved me. But actual sexual contact, in the form of intercourse, was entirely absent from my life in Japan, and the tension of that curious state just about blew me to pieces. Hence, perhaps, the nightly drinking bouts. Deprivation of active sexuality, not uncommon in Japan, where privacy is so expensive, drove me to profound depths of self-consciousness. In my last year in the States I'd traveled incessantly back and forth across the country between the twin insanities of New York and San Francisco and slept in altogether too many people's arms for my own good. Now, in Asia, my promiscuous excess was rewarded by total, involuntary abstinence — yet charged with daily promise of violent lovemaking. The humiliation of this lonesome state provided a real equalizer, or leveler, to the pride I took in my career accomplishments. I was alternately ecstatic and suicidal, manic and depressive. I wondered if most Japanese don't feel something similar.

Sex in Japan! Everyone seems to be interested in it, but no one can quite describe it. (Nobody is interested in sex in India.) Sex in Japan could be the most, or the *least*, personal thing imaginable. I remember the day that the translator of my book *Total Loss Farm*, a distinguished man somewhat older than Kenji and me, came to Kyoto and took us to a night-and-day club *not* mentioned in the tourist brochures. We piled into a taxi and rode to an invisible side street just a few blocks from Kyoto Station where the bullet-train stopped. The cab driver laughed when we told him our destination.

The theater promised little — no marquee, no pictures of what was going on inside — and the admission price was fifteen to twenty dollars per person. The interior consisted of a dark stage and two glass boxes mounted on rails hanging from the ceiling — boxes in which the performers would be moved over the heads of the audience in slow counterclockwise progression. The audience could see everything through the glass floors of these cages. And all the members of the audience were men. The floors were littered with cigarette butts and a thick level of dust and grime — very unlike a normal Japanese theater. The whole place gave off an unwholesome air.

Finally, the lights dimmed and the show began. I by this time expected some kind of striptease exhibition, but what actually followed was more bizarre than that. Essentially it was a parade of naked women, some single and some in pairs, performing abominations on themselves to the background music of a tinny phonograph playing insipid "easy-listening" songs, all to the uproarious approval of the men. The women were older, not very pretty, sometimes a little overweight; worse, their eyes were utterly blank. I felt they were refugees of some devastating collapse in their personal lives. Where were these women's fathers and mothers, families, friends? And why hadn't those families provided a more honorable way to make a living? They expressed no interest in what they were doing or in the men who were watching. Each one did an uninspired, and untalented, dance to the music, stripped, and finally sat on the edge of the stage, back arched, pulling her vagina open and closed inches from the noses of the audience. Some went up into the glass cages in pairs and went through the motions of lesbian love with complete indifference.

I could not "enjoy" the scene in the same way the other men did, but I did feel the wiser, somehow, for having experienced that sad, even heartbreaking "special theater." It made so many things clearer to me. It made me understand, for example, the unendurable pressures which a young woman in Japan feels when she's made a mistake — when she's fallen in love with a foreigner who leaves her pregnant, or given her heart and body to a Japanese man who's faithless, and everyone she knows abandons her. It helped me come to terms with the epidemic in Japan of dead babies found in coin-operated Tokyo lockers — left there by women who'd given birth in complete secrecy for fear of losing their jobs, families, and social standing. So many babies have been abandoned that in recent years the Japanese have created a new word for it — *Ko-in rokka-bebe* ("Go-in-locker baby"). I felt, somehow, an enormous burden of guilt for every GI who'd left a Japanese woman behind him, which, combined with Hiroshima's and Nagasaki's fiery deaths, made me — the flippant American tourist — responsible to repay a debt too heavy for any man. I accepted that responsibility but it drove me crazy.

Taking a kinder view of love in Japan, though — and I *must* at this point to exonerate myself — I did spend a night with a woman who showed me pure delight in our bodies, to the point of orgasm, without our ever joining in conventional intercourse. She was a flower girl, her head full of beautiful scents and powerful songs she wrote and played on the guitar — songs of love lost. We walked around Tokyo by dark hand in hand, hiding from the disapproving eyes of strangers, feeling the delicious danger in our fondness for each other — the possibly ruinous consequences, the shame she would be made to feel if we were found out. We retreated to an apartment she shared with flowers and friends and drank whiskey straight from the Suntory bottle, laughing and talking our funny baby talk. "You like?" "I like!"

She prodded with her delicate fingers into every opening of my body; I loved it, feared it, resisted perhaps in terror, but it was no use; everything came undone before the sun came up. That was only one of many times I shared intimacy with Japanese women — there was an unspeakably beautiful and sentimental artist in Kyoto, and even a high school girl who somehow dreamed that I would take her away with me when I hadn't even noticed her — but that evening comes to mind now, as beautiful as when I spent it.

Beauty is as we make it for ourselves when our environment is as totally devastated as in Japan. Terrifying as the pollution and overcrowding is, every home and every public place has little touches of ornament and art which add a feeling of splendor to the smallest room. A flower arrangement, a rock garden, a bonsai tree — small things which overwhelm the huge ugliness and make the place seem elegant and inspired. Americans tend to think of beauty in gigantic terms — the Rocky Mountains, the great Atlantic and Pacific, the redwood forests and Southwest deserts. Japanese have no, such vistas except in their minds.

Friendship is eternal, if it is real. It adds an evanescent glow to the more sober responsibilities of work, so that who you are with is at least as important as what you are doing. Being alone is close to impossible, so one must guard good friendships and fortify them by building relationships full of implicit understanding (especially when language is a barrier) and special considerations. "I am dreaming that my friend is really my Friend, and that I am my friend's real Friend," Henry Thoreau said.

I was taken to the home of J. Uekusa, seventy-year-old author of eight books and graphic illustrator for many others, and an expert on American literature, jazz, and social movements. I'd heard a lot about Uekusa-san before meeting him, and although I couldn't read his books, I loved looking at his cover photo — which showed him, a tiny old man, wearing a felt hat pulled over one eye, crouching over a cigarette he is lighting, standing on a garish Tokyo street corner. He looked like a private eye in New Orleans, or a jazzman leaving his club at dawn, or some kind of mad hipster midnight poet. He looked wild.

The great Uekusa's house was a small, cozy single-level cottage tucked right beside the Chuo Line train tracks. Every ten or fifteen minutes, when the train from Tokyo Center whisked past, the entire house shook and all conversation was drowned by the noise. Somehow, these loud intervals were delightful and everyone laughed; the blurred commuter train slicing across the window seemed a cheerful reminder of the frantic enterprise going on outside, while we shared high, peaceful communion inside. Every room of the house was full of books — from floor to ceiling on shelves, stacked on their sides on tables, and stored in cardboard boxes underfoot. Most of the books were in English, and most were contemporary; Uekusa had, it seemed, read all the new books by American writers that I had been struggling to find time for. We squeezed ourselves into a room which had been all but devoured by Uekusa's library, and his wife served tea. She also noticed that I was wearing no socks (since I had none) and brought me two pairs of beautiful red and green ones, which I put on and admired. The ad agency guys took lots of photographs and Kenji flattered me outrageously in Japanese; Uekusa-san smiled and enjoyed all the commotion, but when he spoke it was about books, jazz, rock, the American scene. He asked a hundred probing questions about our communal lifestyle, which he'd of course been reading about. For a man who'd never left Japan, he knew more general information about the U.S. than you or I would ever bother to put together.

We began what Uekusa later called, in a newspaper article, "a new kind of friendship." We actually formed a liaison for international literary espionage, and vowed to find B. Traven alive by exchanging clues. Later, he sent me a bright red personal stamp with my name on it fashioned in *kangi* characters — a clever invention since Western names can't be literally translated into ancient *kangi*. Two years thereafter, in 1974, Uekusa came to New York on a book-buying expedition. Every time we've met I've been the happy victim of his quiet charm. Uekusa-san managed, in spite of everything, to lead a contemplative life of the mind in Tokyo. I wondered if that was the privilege of advancing years.

Still another kind of friendship, with a *group* of people, was waiting for us on Sado Island in the Sea of Japan. Because of our background on communes in the U.S., our friends in Tokyo arranged the excursion to Sado to meet a household of young musicians, the Ondekoza Group, who lived and worked together studying the *koto, shakuhachi, jamizen,* and *taiko* — ancient instruments all but forgotten in favor of Western-style music. This "real Japanese commune," we were told, was helping keep the music of Japan alive. Sado Island is the devil's island, rough and mountainous, sitting out to sea a few hours by ferry from Niigata on the western coast, and facing Korea. The very idea of going there was thrilling.

The train for Niigata left Tokyo in midafternoon and arrived in the small but busy port after dark. Paul and I were arguing again, and the trip to Sado turned out to be our last journey together. Kazumasa Satoh, a peppy editorial writer for the *Niigata Nippo* daily newspaper, met us there and got us safely to the boat the following morning. The passenger compartments on the ferry were quite crowded — just long platforms of tatami matting on which everyone sat upright. There were no windows, no view of the water, no fresh air. I consumed a bottle of *budoshi* (grape wine), and attempted to compose an article, but the rocking forced me to abandon it. Up on deck, the cold winter's air felt great and the island of Sado loomed through the clouds like an apparition. Certainly, I felt, this island was to be a different Japan from the mainline population centers.

As the boat inched into Sado's port town, we were startled to hear the booming sounds of a five-foot-wide *taiko* drum bouncing off the mountains all around. Four trim drummers dressed in identical leotards and jackets emblazoned with bold black and white triangles danced around the drum, each pounding it in turn with a great leap. The drum itself was set up on a magnificent wooden platform. The physical strength needed to play such a mammoth drum demanded a musician who could also be an acrobat.

Standing around the drummers, a semi-circle of other members of the Ondekoza Group blew on long reed instruments called *shakuhachi* — they produce a spooky low tone — and one man played a flute. The whole production was so magnificent I didn't even stop to realize that these performers were the same family we had come to visit.

We were royally welcomed to the island, told some stories of its past, and carried off in a van to the commune's fine large wooden house at the foot of a mountain in the interior. From there, we could bicycle or walk to the beaches, where Japanese prisoners once had arrived to be exiled on these shores. My days and nights on Sado were filled with music which invoked the spirits of these ancestors, and of the demon who could be cajoled, on moonlit nights, to dance in old barns in the forest.

The Ondekoza kids — aged eighteen to twenty-three — had all come from big cities in Japan, and all of them had been chosen by their society to participate in the program, which was adequately funded by the same society. In that sense, they were entirely unlike any commune I've ever seen in the U.S.; they were more like what we'd call a military school. They rose at five A.M. every day and ran for six miles behind the group's van, chanting or counting numbers — *ichi, ni, san, shi* — like a mantra. After running came breakfast, and after that practice — hard, long practice — of every kind. They could turn fantastic somersaults on the gymnasium floor, play for hours on wind instruments out of which I, still smoking two packs a day, couldn't even raise a weak moan. At dinner time they all pitched in, in completely happy cooperation, to cook, serve, and clean up after enormous meals. By evening, they sat together to play soft melodies or talk about their progress. No one of them had any active life outside of the demands of their schooling and practice, but all of them seemed happy — even ecstatic.

What marvelous charm, I wondered, could make this group of a dozen healthy, handsome young people — ten men and two women — give up the sex lives, social intercourse, excitements of their native cities for such a hardworking and devoted regime on this spectacular island? Wealth and fame were certainly not incentives — although the group did plan to tour the world with their music once they acquired enough skill by their own rigorous standards.

With every day that passed on Sado, the tensions of life in Tokyo diminished, until after a week I had entered into an actually tripping consciousness and got up every morning feeling like some psychedelic drug had been infused into my bloodstream. The air itself was mysteriously charged with good feelings.

On the last night of our stay, the group announced that we'd been invited to visit the home of one of the oldest men in the village, one of the few who still performed the demon dance which evoked Sado's historic devil-god. The dance was accompanied by huge brightly painted demonic masks, which the dancer lowers over his head, and a monstrously large *taiko* which the drummer *runs* toward and smacks with all the power in his body.

We all went to the barn where the dance would take place after the moon came up. The old structure was full of holes through which the cold wind roared. We lit a charcoal fire and drank a great deal of hot sake with the village teacher, a kind sage whose father had been an important commander of Japanese naval forces in World War II, and who had been killed. This old man's family had been on Sado Island for centuries, and the dance he did was the same dance his ancestors performed in our Middle Ages.

With his mask in place, and all of us taking turns beating the *taiko*, the village teacher began to hop around in the red glowing light of the embers. His pace grew more and more energetic until he was incredibly lifting himself three feet off the floor, spinning around, chanting incomprehensible invocations to the force we hoped to arouse. The idea on Sado had always been that by inviting the devil to show himself through this ritual gathering, men could prevent him from showing himself otherwise. It seemed a remarkably sane and mature attitude, not like the crazed ceremonies of American satanists, and certainly not "evil" in any sense.

And the demon *did* come, though of course I can't describe him. He filled me and everyone in the room with a frantic burning sensation. It was scary and wonderful, dark and cold, mysterious but unmistakably real. This was not the devil I'd seen in monied New York and Tokyo, grinning his hideous inhumane smile. This devil was my friend, an actual creature of God, and the source of my creative energy while I was on the island.

We retreated to the old man's house, where his wife served tea and cookies before a fire and I pondered the experience I'd just gone through. Somehow, I wanted to go home and write poetry to the air.

6 THE LAST few days of our visit to Sado Island produced one of the most dreamlike, spiritual states of consciousness I have ever known. My journey to Japan seemed to reach a turning point with discovery of this haunted place, so different from the heavy neon visions of Tokyo, yet in its way more authentic and uncontaminated by Western imitations. My journey through life itself turned too, as my friend prepared to leave me and I was to go, alone, to walk in India and Nepal in search of some missing part of my heart and soul. I had been decimated by the events of the past year — leaving my farm in Vermont, where I had lived productively for four years; unrequited love; cross-continental homeless wandering; and now this gripping involve-

70

ment with Japan which I would clearly never escape, and which was turning into a great, inevitable search for a new identity. I had noticed that my personal search also reflected a social phenomenon, that others who shared my beliefs and even *looked like me* were also walking around in India, that friends of mine who were also active in the peace movement of the 1960s had turned to gurus and saints. But the experience was still absolutely personal to me, and my awareness that others were sharing the experience meant something only when I retreated to the hotels and cafes where such friends gathered. The loneliness of my mission inescapably came home to me at night, when I crept into bed alone and meditated on my location and my condition.

On the morning we were scheduled to sail back to the main island of Honshu, land of cities and trains, the entire Ondekoza Group scurried into the van, hauling their instruments, including the big *taiko*. I refused to believe, as it would have been presumptuous, that we were going to be sent off with another huge concert, but that is of course what followed. All the musicians set up a chant — "See you again in America!" — which they shouted until they were reduced to a speck against the hills in my eyes. Their drumbeats pounded in my heart.

Niigata on the other side seemed especially gray and crowded. I remember only that we hunted for blocks and blocks for a coffee shop, and the only one we could find was called Blues for You. A tiny cupboard off the street, it had only six seats along a counter, was dark and cool and decorated with posters of New Orleans jazz personalities. The crystal clear audio system played only the blues. I felt, like the singer, that I had a right to sing them. A spell began to settle over me, a spell which later would make my disenchantment with the urban pressures in Japan so great that I had to, and did, move to less crowded places in the woods outside of Kyoto. These new places were certainly civilized and completely urban by our standards, but relatively quiet and isolated by Japanese ones.

The foreign visitor who gets the idea of living "out in the country" in Japan faces few choices of locale if he wants real wilderness. There's Hokkaido to the north, snowy and cold, and Okinawa to the south and west, a semitropical paradise recently vacated by the U.S. Armed Forces. These remote extremes of the country might be considered the safest places to be, since they have not been subjected to such massive environmental mismanagement as the urban areas. But their safety and beauty apparently aren't attractive enough to keep people there, and the population is still moving steadily in the direction of the urban complexes. The empty train we boarded at Niigata was full to bursting by the time it rolled into Tokyo late at night. The in-town train was even more crushed, and once inside we were so jammed into the middle of the car that it was totally impossible to get off at our stop. That left us standing on an open-air platform at the wrong destination, waiting for an equally full subway to carry us back, and I stood by the railing mesmerized by the neon displays. Even Times Square in New York can't compete with Tokyo's Ginza for sheer audacity in neon. The signs moved rapidly every which way, forming pictures and words advertising everything for sale. The Sony tower, with its commanding position over the strip, used one complete side of the building as a moving neon mind-busting sign. Watching all of this, I began to sway and feel slightly nauseated. For the first time, I felt out of the place, apart from it, looking at it with the horror that comes of realizing you're somewhere you don't belong, a place too bizarre and pressured to be good for your health. Perhaps every true New Yorker has had the same feeling, looking out his or her own apartment window. It can best be described as a what-am-I-doing-here sinking feeling in the stomach.

Then the quakes came. The first one struck on the night Creedence Clearwater Revival staged a concert in Tokyo — a night of the full moon. The concert began at six P.M. (the usual time for Tokyo), just at dusk and just as the round yellow moon popped up over the roof tops. "I see a bad moon rising/I feel trouble on the way," the rock group shouted. Words like that sometimes strike me as invocations too serious (and dangerous) to be uttered in public. Kenji and I had just come out of the public bath on Mejiro Dori and, our hair shiny and heavy and our faces pink from the scalding water, had sat down in Aroma (Kenji's favorite coffee joint, a charming gingerbread house with tiny tables and chairs). Paul, Reiko, and other friends were in the concrete-arched concert house. At the stroke of six the room began to sway — at first the normal palpitations of a regular daily earthquake, but then building and growing until the floor and walls were heaving violently, the chandeliers swinging, cups and saucers smashing and falling off shelves. At its peak, it was a terrific force, absolutely terrifying since it left us so helpless. Everyone in the coffee shop sat quietly through the experience, some holding on to fixtures or tables

73

for added support, but nobody running into the street or try-ing to hide. What-am-I-doing-here?

We read in the next morning's paper that the quake had been about 6.5 on the Richter scale and that isolated persons were killed or wounded by heart attacks and falling objects. At that, 6.5, it was not unusual enough to warrant much of a headline. Some of the people in the rock auditorium, dancing to the music of Creedence Clearwater Revival, didn't even feel the ground shake at all!

A week later, a stronger quake — this time in the office of two young guys who put out a monthly "magazine" in English on cassette tapes. That one felt stronger still and I thought it was my time to go. A madonna appeared before me, and I confessed everything. But it stopped.

People in San Francisco are very conscious of the likelihood of suffering from earthquakes, but they don't realize how relatively secure they are compared to a place like Japan — because San Francisco still has *some* space. Some lawns, some back yards, some wide thoroughfares, some parks. Some chance of survival. Houses, some of them, with foundations. Electric and telephone wires attached as secure-ly as possible. Then look down a Tokyo street at the incredi-ble jumble of flimsy buildings heaped on top and alongside each other, linked by a cat's-cradle web of low-slung wires no thicker than a household extension cord. No space to run to, only narrow alleys which are perfect traps for fire and falling debris. Roads out that are choked with traffic every normal weekday. Great holes under the ground, where lightning-fast trains go.

You get the picture now: the place is obviously doomed.

Eventually, as in the past, the tremor will come that flattens the city to ground level, kills many, and displaces the rest. Once I actually saw a city that had suffered such total devastation — while passing through Managua, Nicaragua, in 1973. Hundreds of thousands of people had been forced into the already poverty-stricken countryside and every village was full, with crowds of people loitering in the streets. Hunger was everywhere. My image of Tokyo after such a quake is even stronger, more incredibly miserable. I began to feel foolish to be exposing my self, this fragile body I inhabit, to such a clear and serious danger. In other words, I was scared.

I used to retreat to my friend Kenichi Iyanaga's house at moments of greatest fear. He could make the Japanese spirit of working earnestly in the face of *sure doom* seem elevated, spiritual, and correct. Unlike most people, he wasn't afraid to admit it. So he went every morning, with his American wife Elaine, to the sword master's home. Together they walked to the subway every night with their long swords glinting in the last rays of daylight. They are waiting for the end in a totally gracious way. Their ambition to master the sword is a lifetime calling, and they will surely be practicing it until they die. They lived in the back rooms of his parents' home, where they created an exquisite, peaceful, and comfortable asylum, surrounded by green gardens. They were both as close to saints as any people I've known, and always inspired me to joyful acceptance of my lot.

But Kenichi and Elaine were so busy that it usually took a week-ahead appointment to arrange to see them. In the week of waiting, I'd build up enthusiasm about it until we met, and

I was invariably transported to some high and happy place.

On the night I am thinking of, close to the end of my stay in Japan, I was eating a delicious meal Elaine had prepared, lounging in their room while Kenichi reminded me of the immortality beyond which such things as earthquakes can never reach. "Soon the end will come, and everybody will die. I think sometimes that will be better than this." No monstrous Western ego warring for its own survival gets in the way of a Japanese mind considering the possibility of death.

Martial arts in Japan are as time-honored and traditional as all the other forms of art. Kenichi, descended of the noblest families, was simply following in his ancestors' footsteps with his studies — which combined the skills of swordsmanship with some elusive spiritual program, as if acquiring the disciplines of the sword also gave him the discipline to live a life of correct thought and action. Certainly, for people involved in martial exercises, both Kenichi and Elaine were the most gentle, considerate people in the world. The only killing they did was against their own separatist egos. Japanese have always seen martial arts in educational and religious terms, and their fascination with swords and cutting blades of all kinds is famous. On my return trip from India, I sailed into Yokohama with a German guy named Holger, and his girl friend, who tried to bring an ornate Indonesian sword through port customs and were stopped cold by a complicated code of rules and regulations surrounding swords. The sword was more ornamental than practical, but still it was too long by the rules, and the customs officers were also unwilling and unable to hold the sword aside to be returned to Holger when he left Japan. What they finally did was cut the thing in half and soberly hand Holger the bottom part, which he threw into a garbage can in disgust, swearing at them in German. Kenichi and Elaine had to carry several documents with them at all times, registration papers permitting them to have their swords, which had to be renewed periodically through a heavy bureaucracy.

Elaine had worked and, in a sense, fought for the right to be Japanese, and despite having grown up in New York City, she feared returning to the U.S. more than remaining in Tokyo. After all, you could still walk around Tokyo by night without fear of being robbed, mugged, or raped, she pointed out. She saw so few other foreigners and spoke English so seldom that she was losing her easy command over her native language. (The same thing happened to me to a less dramatic extent; after three months in Japan, I found I was making elementary and awkward mistakes in my English usage.) "Elaine," the American personality, had obviously succeeded in dying and had been replaced by "Mitsuyo," the Japanese name she later adopted.

"I" had to die in Tokyo through the medium of a powerful chemical agent, LSD, experienced in and through a double earthquake of land and mind. By the time we reached Tokyo, both Paul and I — once heavy trippers — had long since abandoned use of acid and gotten bored to death with reading about other peoples' acid trips. But Kenji and his friends had done all the reading without being able to try the drug, and they begged us to have some acid sent to Japan which they could then synthesize and reproduce in a laboratory. So I wrote to a man in New York who'd always had the strongest acid, and he sent half-a-dozen Orange Sunshine tabs packed inside a book and mailed to me in care of my Tokyo publishers.

The book was a popular paperback called *Feel Like a Million*, one of those natural health/natural food primers. Ziggy in New York had carved out some of the interior pages to contain the tablets. The president of the publishing firm in Tokyo opened the package when it arrived, curious to see what new book had come for me, and discovered the acid. He called us at the Chigasaki House full of embarrassment and guilt. "You have received a book from New York," he said, "but . . . (long pause) . . . it's not a book." "Ah so?" "So. I think it's a kind of drug." "Ah so!" He gave us the package with a secret smile.

Kenji was anxious to try it, so we took one tab each while sitting in the Aroma coffee shop one evening just after sundown. No sooner had we swallowed them than the high-pressure NHK producer appeared in the shop, eager to talk to me about a schedule for his documentary. We tried to be serious and responsible, but within ten minutes the acid was rushing up and down our spinal nerve centers and we had to excuse ourselves and run to Mejiro House apartment before the thing got out of hand. The producer simply followed us, unaware of what was going on but still anxious to discuss the TV project some more. Standing on the corner waiting for the green walk light, we felt the buildings sway, the neon lights blur and reshape themselves into frightening images — faces of the dead. Once in the apartment, we collapsed to the floor and began really taking off, alternately laughing hysterically or weeping piteously. The NHK producer sat in the kitchen, trying in vain to resteer the "conversation" back to business and asking repeatedly why we didn't have any liquor in the house. He finally left and Kenji said, "I think he has despair of talking to us tonight." But his departure weighed heavily on both our minds, for we had failed our responsibility toward him. Just before he left, somebody else in the house explained to him that we were tripping, and he asked for some acid to take himself — but I didn't dare give it to him.

The next level of the trip demolished our control and launched us into a nightmare. Kenji was throwing up on the kitchen floor, sobbing, and I felt guilty for having caused the problem, even though I had been asked to do so. I *knew*, after all, the effects of the drug, whereas Kenji did not. I should have politely declined to provide the acid. The worst thing that can happen in Japan is to lose control over one's environment. Now, the ground under me was shaking so fearfully I no longer distinguished between real earthquake and acid-induced earthquake. Everything shook. I was dying fast. Kenji was freaking out. There seemed to be nothing to cling to.

Well, there *was* one thing — the telephone. Kenji got a friend to connect him to Reiko, his partner and strength in the world, who was visiting her mother up north in Sendai. He spoke to her for ten minutes, passionately trying to explain that he was dying and begging for her support; but she couldn't understand, of course, and apparently became angry with him for running up a long-distance phone bill. He hung up more worried than ever. He had that first-time tripper look which says, "What if this thing never goes away, what if this trip never ends?" Time was distorted so that a minute might seem an eternity. I was luckier than Kenji, as I could call Paul, who also knew the LSD experience and would reassure me. "Paul, you have got to come over here and BRING US DOWN!" I pleaded. He said he would come in twenty minutes, "but it will seem like forever to you."

A great number of things happened which I don't remember, then Paul arrived with his sweetheart, Sachiko. I sat with them on the kitchen floor reeling from the impact of the realization that they were, in person, the commingling of East and West, that they would have a child together. She was the same woman I had spent the innocent night with a few weeks earlier. How our lighthearted expedition to Japan was bearing fruit we'd live with forever! I'll never forget the beauty of their faces, bowed together and bright as the sun.

Kenji came out of the bedroom and took Sachiko out into the hall, where they spoke in shouting, in tears, for a few minutes, as if they were having a violent argument. Sachiko came back into the apartment flushed, her eyes burning. She darted right over to me and smashed me across the face with all the force she could gather. Out of the corner of my eye, I saw Paul anxiously removing his eyeglasses as she headed for him and clobbered him over the head. Then she burst into tears.

That blow was what I needed to clear up my mind and heart. After Paul and Sachiko left, Kenji and I retreated to the bedroom and lay there silently holding on to each other in the greatest love. He had had a vision too, of New York City and the beautiful Christine whom I never called on the phone at the studio. Once, he broke down and said, "I told Sachiko to *punch* you!"

"That's all right, Kenji," I replied.

And we fell asleep together like babes.

7 MY SITUATION in Japan was not unlike that of a motherless child, protected under the warm glow, the actually mothering pity and empathy, of adoptive parents. I needed other peoples' help to obtain the necessities of my life, but I also trusted my parents, as any child would, to provide everything I needed. I wanted love, and they gave it. I had never before known love to be a national feeling, but I felt it coming from Japan as a whole. I was let go only as a lover relinquishes his or her mate, with sorrow and some bitterness. A Japanese mother never quite gives up her child, no matter how grown.

The intimacy I felt with Japan was unusual, if not unique, for an American, but I worried whether it might also be perverse or, at best, futile. Try as I might, I would never be Japanese and would never be totally assimilated into Japanese society in the same way that a foreigner can, eventually, come to feel like a full-fledged U.S. citizen. I had to admit, in soul-searching moments, that I was being treated as a rarity, a prize, a special and different person. A guest.

Other Americans in Tokyo told me that their Japanese friends were still treating them in this oversolicitous fashion after ten years or more of acquaintanceship. A Scott Paper executive took us to a restaurant in Tokyo where he ordered several courses in flawless Japanese, at which the waiter cheerfully exclaimed that he spoke Japanese so well! "Do you know that guy's been telling me I speak Japanese so well for fifteen years?" he groaned in English loud enough for all to hear. This poor executive rode on the commuter trains three hours a day, had a wife and house in the suburbs, and complained that while he couldn't stand the U.S., he and his family lived in total exile in Japan. But he wrote beautiful poetry which was published in Tokyo and Vermont, and stayed home at night, I presume, meditating on trees and stars, because he was a sensitive man under the burdens of an uncreative work environment, and he suffered the age-old frustration of the unrecognized artist.

I was struck by the fact that all the Americans I met who were living and working in Japan were carrying on an elaborate love-hate relationship to the place. On the one hand, they had chosen to exile themselves, sometimes at great sacrifice and expense; and on the other, they all held the place in some degree of contempt. A highly competitive marriage has been going on between the two nations since

83

the end of the war, with Japan playing the role of wife. She has accepted and transformed our energy, turning it into a new thing unique to Japan — so that when Americans look at Japanese society they are seeing their own image reflected in a prismatic mirror that bends and twists the shapes.

The word for "foreigner" is *gaijin*, which, spoken in a certain tone, can be as pejorative as the word "Jap" in our own usage. Whatever else went down, *gaijin* remained *gaijin*, "out of the family," and I realized it would take some years more for this extraordinarily homogeneous Japanese racial identification to break down. I resented this block to my ultimate bond with my new home, but I could not forget that I was adopted, an orphan. I owed gratitude but not loyalty. Deep in my heart, I had not burned all my bridges to the past as I thought. Being *gaijin* was thus my special attractiveness and my major fault at the same time, and in time I was homesick for a world full of people speaking my language.

What had begun as an adventure had assumed aspects of duty, mission. When I asked myself *why* I was going through all the mental turmoils necessary to cope with Japan, I realized it was my *job*. I was my own boss and client, and my goals were to achieve humility, patience, and the spirit of hard work.

With humility I'd never want more than I could get; with patience everything would come my way eventually anyway; and with the spirit of hard work I'd be too busy to have to think about it.

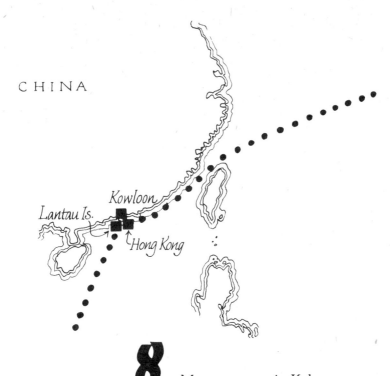

CHINA

Kowloon

Lantau Is.

Hong Kong

8

MY LAST NIGHT in Kobe was strangely secure, comfortable, private, sad, and hopeful. In the morning, I'd be out on the rolling sea which separates clumps of land, nations, people, languages, and colors — the sea which great airborne jets ignore while sailors of the world still toss in their bunks, undisturbed by the sight of anything but water and sky. I brought a book, just one, from Japan — Mishima's devastating novel *Forbidden Colors*, which I'd later tear apart in Bangkok and stuff full of Thai marijuana as an air-mail gift to friends in Tokyo. The first Kobe port-side hotel I visited was too expensive for my dwindling supply of yen, but the desk clerk kindly made a reservation for me at a nearby, cheaper hotel — which itself was still luxurious by my standards. I richly enjoyed the privacy of my final hours there. I masturbated in clean white sheets, something I'd never had the privacy to do in Japan! I dreamed of Hong Kong, a week away by Polish freighter, and imagined getting high in Chinese opium dens.

An otherworldly sensation came over me. I was plainly going to succeed in my effort to leave Japan, an achievement for which I'd been striving against mighty odds. But *could* I get away simply by moving my physical body across the watery planet to Hong Kong, or would all the things I'd left unfinished in Japan haunt every step I took? What of tender friendships about to blossom? What about the projected NHK television documentary, the Sony video-cassette tour? Wouldn't Mrs. Nagamine be upset to learn that I'd left without saying good-by after she'd worked so hard to find me a house? (She later charged Paul ten thousand yen for a cigarette burn in the tatami, and I suspect the money involved was far less agonizing than our shame over having misused the tatami, as all foreigners are said to do.) The gnomish master of the Aroma coffee shop would get married and I'd miss the party. Would I lose contact with the vital reinforcement of my Tokyo society? Paul would fly to New York with Sachiko, where they'd marry, long before I returned; I felt helpless to express my concern for their fate. I felt myself slipping away, again, from the familiar psychodramas of my life and my friends' lives and into a greater solitude than I'd previously endured.

Everything conspired, as before, to force me to leave when I did. It was a sunny April day and I still felt the absence of that intangible love higher than names which would resolve

86

my splintered life and make my heart whole. Of course I wondered, again, whether I might be running away from the love and peace I craved, and whether I might not do better at finding myself by just staying put. These rational arguments had been going on in my head for years, and never ultimately persuaded me to stay or go; the born wanderer will use 90 per cent of his time in traveling for just staying alive, as if the moving itself were work enough to sustain him. I knew some inspiration, something outside of myself which could blow "me" away, was waiting for me in India. Too much self-consciousness in Japan had made me oversensitive, weepy, sometimes self-pitying, mawkishly sentimental, alternately ecstatic and miserable. I longed for a life of uninterrupted Satisfaction and Bliss. Since my best efforts at amour, with either sex, had proved too much for partners or for me, I imagined I might find happiness in a celibate and spiritual life.

What makes us think we can find perfect serenity and bliss anyway? My parents would not have believed such a thing possible short of heaven; in trying to find it on earth, I was presuming the existence of a God within us. As vague as that faith may seem, it sustained me. I knew myself, on that freighter utterly alone churning through the South China Sea, to be only a pawn in somebody's game, and I resented and accepted it. I came at last to the very edge of my faith and found I could never quite relinquish it.

Stepping from Japan to Poland-in-transit to China made me feel cut off from familiar protocols, insecure and antisocial. Japanese people do not adapt well to foreign environments, according to a common theory, but I've known personally some glowing exceptions. I found myself unable or unwilling to accept Poland on its own terms; the food seemed too heavily carbohydrated (bread, potatoes) and fatty (sliced meats, butter) and too little else; the service was miserable — couldn't buy a pack of cigarettes because the ship couldn't change a traveler's check; the ship's officers were stoic bureaucrats and the crew, though friendly, were too seldom seen. I wrote a long incriminating suffering letter to Paul. I felt I'd made a mistake in boarding the ship, but it was too late. Every day took me further from Japan and closer to my rendezvous with Hong Kong. I had become so infected with the work spirit and the drive for accomplishment that I feared returning to Japan until I'd completed my mission in India, however long it took. I would return triumphant or not at all. Thinking of all the people who'd seen me off, I realized I was just as good as my promise.

By the final day of the crossing we were spotting the barren green-black rock islands jutting from blue calm waters around Hong Kong. Some of these craggy reefs had signs of human life but most did not. One red junk appeared, a flimsy funny tub with a big scalloped white sail, bobbing and dipping perilously in the wave from the ship. Hundreds of other junks gradually joined it, surrounding our ship, but their owners went on fishing in apparent obliviousness. I stood on the deck in sunglasses and shorts, shirtless for the first time in a season, and gave that Polish tub my most withering curse. Cursing is an unpleasant thing to do, usually arises out of spite and seldom does anyone any good. In this case, it seemed to spark a fire in the engine room. Suddenly all hands were running around the deck with fire

88

hoses, the engine cut out completely, and the passengers were all transferred to a spunky Chinese motor launch topped with green striped awning and driven into bad Hong Kong harbor. I was filled with cynical delight.

Diabolic Hong Kong! Stunning, overwhelming, perched on the sea and sky, it can be beautiful but is always cruel. Here is the major center of hard drug traffic in Asia, the supply outlet for kidnapped babies sold to childless couples in Taiwan, the manufacturing capital for counterfeit money, cheap sundries, watches that don't work, pornography, Kung Fu movies, spy secrets. Here, it seemed, every shred of dignity had been sacrificed to money and even the most wealthy shopkeepers were thieves and liars. The wind whipped across my face as I rode the nickel ferry back and forth between Hong Kong and Kowloon, sitting on a wooden bench under signs that said Do Not Spit and Watch Out For Pick-Pockets in crude letters. Pretty girls with sincere smiles sell airline tickets for flights which will never be scheduled; grinning well-dressed dope dealer/con man drives you up dark alleyway; wasted smack man in a tent-shanty gives first-timer tastes for free and makes further orders progressively more expensive. Hoteliers double the rates for unsuspecting newcomers, prostitutes slouch and chatter, some neighborhoods are so dangerous it's considered suicide to wander there. Hong Kong is a mean town, as everybody knows but few could really imagine. Her jazzy streets and people with sidelong glances only hurt my eyes.

However boring Poland may have been, it was always safe and secure; Hong Kong seemed a major risk by comparison. The people were rushed, curt, overworked, pale, and tense.

The bars were at least vaguely suspicious, the food not always fit to eat. I passed the first night in a hotel bar near my room, which I shared with a Danish couple chance-met. The bar was furnished in modern, dark and expensive, and a fantastic obese black man played the piano and sang "The Impossible Star" like an angel to my drunken mind. In the room there were only two beds, and the Danish guy jumped back and forth from his girl friend's bed to mine, laughing, "I'm a Gemini, I can't decide!" He'd just hold our hands and talk for a while, then leap away. Eventually my conversations with other foreigners met in public places or at the American Express office led me to the cheapest "hotel" for freaks in town, the Wing On Travel Service — where a narrow bunk in a room packed with a dozen men cost fifty cents a day. The entire travel service consisted of two rooms on the eleventh floor of a decrepit building behind the Bank of America. There was an elevator on which everyone left graffiti and rode in silence. The sleeping room, although partitioned into sleeping and living spaces, was seldom completely quiet or dark. Nobody got much rest in the Wing On.

Surrounding the building were many stalls — tents, really — where tea, coffee, and food were ostensibly served while clusters of emaciated men smoked powdered heroin packed in the ends of cigarette butts in the back room. Behind one of these stalls, smoking with the leader while the heat washed over us and sirens wailed, was Nowhere, lost, so far gone I'd never come back, I thought, so confused I'd given up trying to understand. Oh, periodically, lying in my bunk in the Wing On and staring at the ceiling while listening to my Australian roommate's cassette recorder playing Leon

Russell, I'd suddenly wonder what in hell I was doing with my youth, my life, why I was wasting away in this hole. But the smoke obliterated my resolve.

It makes some people more comfortable to imagine that young Americans with so many resources allow themselves to sink into a morass in Asian (or African, Middle-Eastern, European, etc.) slums out of a quest for adventure, a thirst for the exotic, some youthful madness that must be worked off. I can only admit that in my case I felt I'd been given no alternative but to follow this path; I did not exactly choose to live these experiences, but, more accurately, *found myself* living them, sometimes to my own surprise. I simply let go and the life carried me off. (I didn't resist too much.)

British people in Hong Kong, many of them, acted like they owned the place, which in political fact they do. I found it hard to believe that this city of ten million industrious Chinese really needed British management. The sight of a fat pink Englishman being pulled up a hill in a rickshaw by a sweating coolie made my blood boil. As nervous and unhappy as the natives seemed, the British were somehow worse for their smugness and snobbish camaraderie amidst the rubble. The more I knew of Hong Kong, the less I cared for it and the more wary I became.

Finally, it was only letters and money I'd arranged to have come in the mail, but which hadn't arrived, that kept me waiting in Hong Kong. I'd had enough, but didn't care to leave my mail behind since I couldn't be sure it would be forwarded. Little considerations like that never mean anything in America, where we have "many cold drinks" and a nearly perfect post office!

My tourist map indicated a daily ferry run to the island called Lantau, about an hour's trip. I left the city on that windy ferry, drinking Seven-Up on her passenger deck, exposed to the weather. We threaded in and out of barren islands until reaching Silvermine Bay, port village of Lantau Island.

The island was awesome in appearance — enormous black hills looming over a tiny fishing village and beach. A few hundred peasants lived in the village, lined with mud lanes, and the island was otherwise barren and empty — except for three monasteries, a rehabilitation center (prison) for heroin addicts, and a colony of lepers. I took the road — there was only one — through the village and out into the fields stretching up the mountainside. All the people stayed in their houses. I didn't stop until I reached the road's end at a large homestead and farm. The farm dog came running from the house to the fence, where I stood waiting, and growled fiercely at me. Where I found an unfriendly dog there was usually an unfriendly person nearby.

A man appeared at the door to the house and shooed me away with his hand. I stayed. He got angry and began shouting and waving me away. But I didn't move. Finally he approached me, obviously very agitated. When he was ten feet from me I saw his leprous face eaten by running sores, and turned slowly away.

The beach was a beautiful crescent kissed by rushing waves and blessed by peace and quiet. I decided to sleep there if nothing better was possible, rather than return to Hong Kong. A twisting path led up and around so many hilltops from which I could see miles, so many hidden treasures of temples and caves, so much hardship, so much beauty. The villagers were innocent and pleasant, not like the city folk. I finally sat down in the outdoor beach café with a cold beer and a cigarette.

I noticed out of the corner of my eye a tall, stout white man with flowing white hair and a goatee, wearing a somewhat ludicrous pair of madras shorts and an African-style pith helmet. He ambled. I remember thinking he had come out of some Tennessee Williams play. Dr. Archibald Yow, "cosmologist," sat down beside me and said, "You're not one of those devils in human form, are you?"

Dr. Yow, born in South Carolina sixty-three years before, had made it to California and finally to Hawaii, where he lived on the beach until the "bourgeoisie" arrived. He sailed to Hong Kong with two trunks weighing hundreds of pounds each, stuffed with the manuscripts of his lifelong un-published work, *The Book of the Cosmos*. He was also the president and sole member of the Society of the Cosmos, which I promptly joined. He was the only guest of the only hotel on Lantau Island, the Seaside House, where I "registered" by paying two dollars for four days. Our rooms were not "adjoining," but were exposed to each other by the airspace over the eight-foot wall which came far short of the ceiling. They were not rooms, but tombs.

Dr. Yow and I spent nearly all our time together after that first encounter. Unfortunately, I can't recall even a single principle of the society, but I did learn enormous lessons from Yow's conduct. He was not what people would call a pleasant man, and thus had his privacy secured. He was rude and insulting to the Chinese, calling them chinks, bellowing

93

in indignation when offered chopsticks to eat with, finally knocking a village man down. He had a terrible temper and was prone to outbursts of indignation over philosophical points. His personal life seemed directed at a mother still living in the South, toward whom he felt enormous guilt. He planned to hire a local fisherman to build him a Chinese junk for about a thousand dollars on which he could sail out of Hong Kong — for he had originally been given only three days on his visa by a suspicious customs officer; and, having already overstayed his visa by months, he feared arrest and imprisonment if he attempted to leave on his own passport. He was a prisoner of Lantau Island, and wanted only a boat with which to sail off, trunks and all, for India. He had some grass which he'd brought from Hawaii — and grass was just as hard to find in Hong Kong as in Japan — and would roll me toothpick-thin joints whenever I'd plead my need. He was a great scholar of the occult disguised in the earthly form of a reprehensible bitter old man. I became determined to learn everything he could teach me, because he was not very different from myself.

Like me, he got stoned, drank, wrote books, sensed auras, traveled on the astral plane, and was lazy. I wondered if he were an image of my future. I felt he must be lonely. "Loneliness is weakness," he'd snarl. He was one of those rare practitioners who show us the right path by showing the wrong.

And a certain German monk who lived not in but by the grand temple of Pin Lo on the mountain, was another. I encountered him for the first time on one of my ferry runs to the city for smack, which Dr. Yow had taken to joining me in. On the return trip to Lantau, I happened to climb down the ship's stairs in defiance of the sign reading, "First class passengers not allowed on the downstairs deck." There, this thin monk was sitting in a pile of rice sacks, grinning at me and picking his teeth with a toothpick. "Sit down," he said.

I had heard stories about this fellow in the village. He was said to have been born in Germany but had joined the Pin Lo monastery ten years before, and also spoke excellent Chinese. I had once ridden the local schoolboys' bus up to the monastery hoping to speak with him but he was not there. He had piercing blue eyes and spoke loudly and boldly.

The monk too had a cynical attitude toward my odyssey. But he knew my name, where I was coming from and going to, *and why*, without my having to tell him anything. He warned, cryptically, that a "mungo" in China is a "kind of snake." He foresaw that I'd run out of money in India. But beneath his stern face there was undeniable sympathy that comes of recognizing a brother caught in one's own plight.

For we were all the same — A. Yow, the German monk, and me. We were seekers living out days and nights on that same outcasts' island. I never knew whether Dr. Yow was conscious of his appalling manners, and using them as a shield against the unfair and unappreciative public, or whether he never saw himself as I did. Certainly, I believed I could be like him in my sixties — still wandering, annoyed by other people's presence, carrying trunks of manuscripts — but I felt sorry for him and myself. And the monk — I too could voluntarily shed all things of the world and live in a cave on Lantau Island, but only if the world started treating me with less love and respect than it had in the past. The alternatives these two teachers offered left me feeling there must be something more; and when I had gained what I could from the two of them, I was free to leave. I flew some shady Korean charter to Bangkok for seventy dollars.

British troops arrived to practice war maneuvers on the island the morning I left, and Dr. Yow and I got into a terrible altercation over it. Their helicopter knocked down the beach café's awning on our heads while we were eating breakfast, and I flew into a rare tantrum, screaming "Fuck the British!" at the top of my lungs. Dr. Yow screamed back at me for being, as he put it, nationalistic! We finally reassembled the awning and left the argument unresolved as my boat pulled in and I rushed away. The island receded in my perspective, finally hiding behind a cloud on the horizon. I left behind there, like the lepers and former addicts, a shocking amount of poison excreted, as it were, from my soul. I dripped the blood of failure on those bleak hills, deprived my body of food, put myself down as hard as I'd ever been able to do, gave myself too little credit, and generally pined away. But I left certain that the worst was over and pleased that I'd survived a kind of acid test.

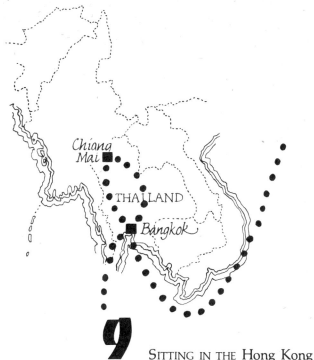

9   SITTING IN THE Hong Kong
airport, I went through a frightening heroin withdrawal.
Three weeks on that awful white stuff, less satisfying as I
used more of it, had left me weak and confused but determined to escape. A stack of letters, not including the money I
was expecting from Tokyo, arrived for me at American Express, and I opened and read them while waiting for my
plane to Bangkok. My correspondents probably couldn't
realize the powerful emotional effect their letters would have
on me — here was one from a former girl friend with whom I
could have led a decent married life; one from a man friend
at my farm in Vermont, telling of the spring planting;
another one from good friends in San Francisco, detailing

who had moved to Marin County and who had published a new book. I cried over these letters so publicly that people moved away from me in the waiting lounge, perhaps even fearful of me. I cried because the letters represented alternatives to my difficult path to India which I couldn't reverse although I wanted to. I missed all those friends, and their sincere offers to take me back, as it were, only made me feel worse. Even surrounded by their love, I was missing some vital, intangible spirit which would make my life worth living. I was missing myself. The Korean charter plane to Bangkok was announced, and I tore up all the letters and stuffed them in the nearest litter can with a final sigh, then marched myself to the departure gate and flew to Thailand in a dreamlike state, the result of malnutrition, smack, and loneliness.

As we left the plane and strolled across the Bangkok airfield to the terminal, the differences between Thailand and Hong Kong were immediately striking. Heat and darkness and feelings of some mysterious charm overwhelmed me. The airport was old and musty, not modern, and the city of Bangkok low lying and dark, not jazzy and full of neon. The customs man scarcely looked at my passport, and soon I was caught in the crowd of arriving passengers in the baggage room, trying to figure out the confusing maze of hotel directories and taxi drivers offering their services. A young Australian freak in Hong Kong had given me the name of the Thai Song Greet Hotel in Bangkok as the central gathering place for people of "our kind," and I asked the driver to take me there. He spun around in his seat and I caught his sharp, black, beautiful dancing eyes and the gleam of his teeth smiling broadly. "Thai Song Greet! OK, boss, number-one hotel! Number-one hotel!" He laughed and laughed in the most infectious way, and I got the point that this hotel was going to be some dump, but I started laughing anyway and couldn't stop myself. The driver was a short, stout fellow with a baby face and a way of talking I could only call cute. All Thai people struck me as so sweet, so "cute," and so naturally happy (Thailand is called the Land of Smiles) that from the first I wanted to hug them up and hold them tight. In some ways, I believe they saved me from sure self-destruction.

The taxi driver seemed in no hurry to get going to the Thai Song Greet. He was waiting for more passengers to fill his cab, but I assumed he was just taking his time. He asked if I'd like to know a Thai song; I said yes, and he sang it over and over for me until I got the hang of it and we sang together at the top of our lungs, beating the upholstery and stomping the floor of the car in rhythm. At the end of every verse, he'd laugh and applaud me. He also played a hide-and-seek game with his eyes, in which he'd turn around, look me in the eye for an instant, break into uncontrollable giggling, and turn back to the steering wheel. After he recovered, he'd do it again and start giggling again. When the new passengers arrived — a nervous group of West Germans who didn't trust the driver to handle their baggage — he and I were delirious. The taxi wouldn't start, no matter how hard we tried, and that made us laugh even more, while the Germans stewed in disgust and anxiety. The driver and I got out and pushed it to a start, assisted by a couple of other Thais who ran over to help.

The streets of Bangkok were steaming and lush — tall palm trees lined the broad ribbons of the major avenues, the narrow side lanes were crowded in by vegetation, the wooden shacks open to the night air. People slept in hammocks in their houses and yards even in the center of town, and a silver canal jammed with houseboats and rafts glowed in the moonlight as it flowed lazily to the sea. Ancient walls and tiled façades of palaces activated some indescribably lovely part of my memory — my incarnational, cellular memory — of old Siam.

The Thai Song Greet Hotel was a dusty old building open to the street, just off the main square where shops and people and buses and cars filled the air with riotous activity. All the shops, like the hotel, were completely exposed to the hot night air, and people sat around drinking tea or beer in their shorts or pajamas. The lobby of the hotel was a restaurant presided over by a fat, roaring good-natured man who spat great clumps of phlegm onto the floor every few minutes. His wife and children served up plates of rice with sauces and stews — bits of fish, meat, fruit, bread swimming in fiery hot spices. All the food was displayed openly and the cooking conditions would certainly seem unsanitary to any Westerner, but the crowd of long-haired stoned-out freaks lounging there ate every bite with enthusiasm, and so did I. I ate and ate and drank cold Seven-Up on ice until I was full to burping and realized I'd just eaten more in one sitting than in three long weeks in Hong Kong. The rest of my stay in Thailand was like that; I ate and drank with gusto, sometimes in the face of incredulous Thais who believed their food to be inedible to Americans as a result of their ex-

100

perience with disdainful GIs. If I smoked some Thai marijuana, probably the best marijuana in the world, I'd eat twice as much as usual. And laugh all the time.

I ordered a room in the Thai Song Greet, and was taken to a dark cubbyhole without windows which had one narrow, dirty bed and no bath or other comforts. There was a cold shower stall down the hall used by all the residents. The door to the room locked from the outside with an oversized padlock that barely fit its hinges, but it didn't lock at all from the inside. Not five minutes after I'd arrived in the room, a knock came on the door and a painted woman entered. She was in her thirties, perhaps, had full long black hair, sparkling eyes, and a nice smile, but had ruined it all with a gaudy dress and too much make-up — blood red lipstick, thick rouge, eye shadow, nail polish. She looked like some caricature of an Asian whore one might have imagined as a bit player in a Charlie Chan movie. Exhausted as I was, I didn't even realize that she *was* a whore, and I kept trying to explain to her that she had the wrong room. She left in disgust, swinging her purse through the air in an arc. Five minutes later *another* woman arrived, and I got the point. The third one who came was accompanied by the fat hotel manager, shouting, "What's the matter, you don't like this one either?" I explained politely that I wasn't in the market for *any* whore, and he threw up his hands as if to say he couldn't understand my attitude! Then we laughed about it and I went to bed surrounded by cockroaches so big they seemed to be walking on stilts around the room.

Unfortunately, the noise from the street below not only penetrated the walls of my room but actually made them

101

shake. Zombied as I was, I couldn't sleep, so I took a long walk around Bangkok in the early hours before dawn. The big parks, gracefully sloping roof tops of the alabaster palace, and even the poor thatched roof tops of huts and shops seemed divinely beautiful after my exile in Hong Kong and on Lantau, the lepers' island.

A young boy hanging out with his friends near a gasoline pump shouted to me as I passed. "Hey, where you going?" He grinned so broadly that his teeth shone in the reflected street lamp. I was too tired to answer, and anyway I didn't *know* where I was going, so I walked on without acknowledging him. To my complete astonishment, he ran up the street to me, hopped in front of my path, and began dancing up and down feigning boxing blows with both fists. Still smiling and jumping up and down, he said, "You no speak, I BOXING you!" I broke down, put my arm around him and tried to tell him where I was going. He hugged me in return. And I learned a lesson which stayed with me throughout the time I was in Thailand — I learned to say yes to everything and to *touch* everybody.

Late that night I found a twenty-four hour coffee shop in an expensive hotel where the waiter wanted to take me home with him to meet his mother. I wasn't ready for that, but I did get him to promise to get me some grass — which he never did, but I couldn't be angry. He, like so many others, became emotionally involved with me and came to see me at my various hotel rooms.

I got my first taste of the legendary grass from a kind prostitute in a bar, who had her teen-age son run down the street and fetch me some. I had entered the bar in a hot, despondent condition, and she came to sit by me, as Thai whores will, begging me to buy her a drink, which I did. When she offered her services and I refused, she said in astonishment, "But if you don't want me why did you buy me a drink, honey?" I replied, "Because you *asked* me for one." (As I said before, I could not say no to anything. My path was one of total surrender.) She asked where I was staying and, hearing the name of the very cheap hotel, she saw that I could not really afford the drink I bought her. Next thing I knew, her son scurried in from the street and presented me with a thick wad of newspaper, inside which I found the most hallucinatory green cannabis I've ever known. I won't labor the point any further, but to a person who enjoys smoking pot as much as I do, the experience of Thai stuff — which was so plentiful that I ended up with sacks full of it for free — gave the place an otherworldly, paradisiacal quality. The first joint I smoked, in my fan-cooled room at the Atlanta Hotel, the "other" hippie hotel in town, left me totally paralyzed for hours, my head seemingly separated from my body, and I dreamed outrageous fantasies of color, sound, smell, ideas, visions of my Lord, earth beneath my toes, love and laughter in my heart. Sudden waves of paranoia. Stunning awareness of the slaughter across the field, in Vietnam our neighbor, which at that time was under the heaviest U.S. bombing in history. Desire to give away my material resources to everyone in need. Waves upon waves of the high from Thai.

Seen from the consciousness of political ideology and plain common sense, Thailand has many serious problems. But they do not prevent the population in general from running around in apparent glee, and they couldn't extinguish the sheer delight I took in the people and place. Among the sobering problems was the war in Vietnam, of course. Thailand seemed to profit from it and officially sided with the Americans; Bangkok was full of diversions specifically created for the U.S. soldier and his money. I made a good profit at the local race track on a horse called Why Worry?

Thailand has more public executions than any other nation — thousands of Thais turn out to watch and applaud the national executioner, an obese jolly fellow who became something like a sports star or popular hero. He got paid by the head, around fifty dollars for every enemy of the state that he shot.

The food is plentiful, the land very rich, but it does make most Westerners constipated — a refreshing change from the diarrhea you'll get elsewhere.

The buses in Bangkok don't have mufflers or any space to sit down; worse, they don't completely stop at the curb so that you have to jump on and off, sometimes clinging to a pole with one hand while the bus goes roaring off as fast as it can; and finally, they play chicken with other buses, driving furiously toward a head-on collision, then ducking off to the side at the last possible moment while the passengers cheer. The people have a different attitude toward death and danger than ours: they laugh at it.

Which is not to say that the Thais have no compassion. In fact, they run over with it. Their ways of being with each other seemed intensely personal and loving compared to the distant, don't-touch protocols of Japanese and American society. My friend Steve Lerner came down with hepatitis in

India and was nursed back to health over a year in Thailand, as a charity patient who might as easily have lacked a name and nationality.

I wanted to go to North Vietnam, as I'd met some North Vietnamese in a conference arranged by the peace movement back in 1967. (The conference was held in a small village in Czechoslovakia, and I remembered that the Vietnamese had come eighteen days by train through the Soviet Union to spare the expense of flying.) At some other time, I might have been able to enter. But at the moment I presented myself, conditions in North Vietnam had never been so dangerous. The papers I needed to proceed there never arrived, so I decided to go up into the hills of northern Thailand, over into Laos, and all around the area, to get a better feeling for the countryside. Having packed up my things to leave Bangkok, I stopped at the Star Café by the main post office for a last cup of coffee. I intended to hire a boat to take me up the canal on the first leg of the journey north to Chiang Mai.

But the waiter who brought the coffee asked where I was going and, hearing my plan, begged to accompany me to the jungles in the north. He had a girl friend there whom he wanted to marry, he said, and he'd take me to her village, where we could stay in her parents' house while exploring. He took me home (to meet his mother) and tried to convince me to pay extra to bring several of his friends along to Chiang Mai, but I didn't have enough money with me, so "John" (as he called himself) and I went alone, choosing an all-night bus as the least expensive way to travel.

The bus trip was total murder on our bodies, a crowded,

jerking, pounding experience. The passengers sat six abreast on chairs meant for four, with all their bags jammed into the aisle so that no one could move. But when the bus stopped at occasional rest areas, strongholds of the highway where soldiers guarded the night and watched for guerrillas, I felt I was out in the greatest, thickest wilderness in the world. The stars blessed us and the sounds of American pop music blared through scratchy sound systems in the inky night. The number-one song at the time went, "I want to know, have you ever seen the rain, coming down on a sunny day?"

In Chiang Mai, an ornate bicycle-driven carriage with a bright awning top took us through the magnificent town at dawn. We stayed at a plain hotel and set out later in the day for the village. We walked for three days in all, to and from the girl friend's house and through a number of tiny villages where, John said, the people had never seen a white man. They stared at me in silence. All the places, and the whole journey, was like floating through a timeless universe of impossibly green vegetation, peaceful villages, and old men smoking on porches, seeing far. No young men were around. And John's girl friend had already gone south and married another. He was so sad I had to hold his hand all the way back to Bangkok. We walked along dusty roads under the blazing sun wondering what would become of us. We got back to Chiang Mai and blew the last of my money on a more comfortable train ride back to the city.

While sitting in the Thai Song Greet restaurant one hot afternoon, I was approached by a Chinese youth who called *him*self Mark. He was selling International Student Cards that his uncle, a printer, had made up. They looked exactly like the student cards issued by a legitimate international students' union in London, except for the inferior quality of the paper and some typographical errors which would be noticed only by somebody who spoke English as a native language. Using one of these counterfeit cards, even a middle-aged hobo could pose as a "student" and take advantage of huge discounts on train travel and other services. The scheme worked particularly well in India, where the cumbersome bureaucracy loved to honor special permits and documents.

Mark couldn't sell me a card, though I later bought one in Katmandu, but I did go with him to his uncle's print shop in the street in Bangkok. Using Mark as my translator and guide, I gave the Chinese printer the manuscript of a book Paul and I had written together enroute to Japan. Called *Right to Pass*, it was kind of a pamphlet full of Zenish aphorisms. The book was printed to resemble a U.S. passport in size and color, and the back cover was emblazoned with the motto we found on a Boise Cascade Corporation sign posted in the redwood forests of northern California: "Right to pass is by permission only and subject to control of owner." The inside back cover bore the legend "500 copies Made in Thailand by Mark."

Printing the books in the sun and grit of the Bangkok street was one of the toughest jobs I undertook in Thailand. The printers didn't know a word of English and made many mistakes which had to be redone. But they worked patiently and with intelligence, and the final product is as handsome a book as you could produce for $125 anywhere in the world. I distributed the books free to many of the people I met on my way thereafter.

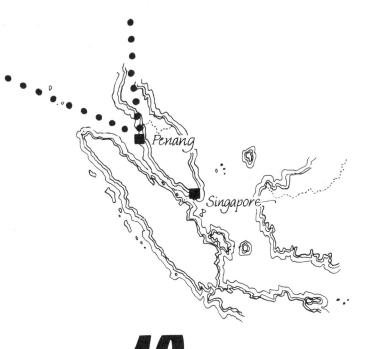

Penang

Singapore

10

AS MY THREE-WEEK tourist visa
neared expiration, I kept devising excuses to remain in
Thailand and southeast Asia in general, prolonging my inevitable departure for India and enjoying the fruits of the
earth and sea. My marijuana stash got so large I started mailing it out to friends in Japan and America packed in books;
I'd cut out the inner section of perhaps a hundred pages, fill it
with grass, and leave a perfectly normal looking book, with
all four sides intact, then wrap it as a gift with one end open
for postal inspection and send it book rate air mail. I had
some sweet, giggling shop girls make a flamboyant silk shirt,
which I sent to a friend in Tokyo, carried by a Swiss engineer
chance-met. Eventually, I found myself swimming in

Bangkok society, meeting old friends on the street and knowing the waiters in all the gathering places. And feeling a bit too familiar. My mission, after all, was not yet completed, and having too much of a good time troubled my conscience. I sincerely believed that some spiritual master was waiting for me in India, that the good time I would find there would be actual bliss. Yet I felt real pangs of tender regret about leaving Bangkok.

Smart travelers arrange all their visas before leaving home, but of course I wasn't sane enough to have thought of it. I invariably got my visa for the next country on my path just at the point when I was ready to proceed. Generally, you can buy a visa in ten minutes for a few dollars, but the Indian consulate in Bangkok made the visa to India a real privilege. The office was open only a few hours a day and in no case would consider granting a visa on the same day it was requested. You had to produce three photographs of a particular size, mountains of personal documents, and be interviewed about why you wanted to go to India! I lost another three days fulfilling all the qualifications on the long Form of Application for an Alien Desiring to Proceed to India. And when I told the consul I was searching for my guru, he looked at me as if I were crazy. But he stamped my passport and signed it. It was the first of many stamps in my passport from Indian bureaucrats — three full pages of stamps for having bought traveler's checks, for having entered or left certain provinces, for having bought a ticket on a boat. Indian bureaucracy is formidable but also confused and meaningless; a permanent record is made of *everything*, but is never referred to thereafter.

I chose to leave Thailand by train to Malaysia, the lush peninsula stretching to the south and curving its arm around to encompass the free port of Singapore. In the afternoon heat at the Thai Song Greet, I sat with Mark and John and scores of others drinking and making our good-bys. My train pulled out at four P.M.; at midnight the Thai Song Greet was busted by national police and sundry people carried off for possession of drugs. I saw a photo of my friends on the front page of another passenger's morning newspaper when I woke up in Haad Yai, a tiny border town in the south. Once again unconscious decisions, just following the signs, had led me out of danger. I wondered why.

The Thai train was a joy in itself. Its wooden interior and stuffed upholstery made it seem and ride like an old-time western train in Wyoming. And out the open windows you could see vast green jungles and smell the perfume of tropical flowers carried on the heat waves. Vendors sold cold drinks through the windows at station stops, and all the people shared their food. Sitting there amidst Thai families with their box lunches, I felt blessed.

The border formalities at Malaysia were cordial and simple, and we all changed trains to continue the journey down to Penang, the western port city of Malaysia and a temple of Islam. We got off the train at its final stop and boarded a foot-passenger ferry to Penang, which gleamed in the sunset like an African dream, with its mosque roof tops and low-slung white buildings. And it hummed with the resonance of thousands of old men's voices chanting to Allah at sundown. Bells were ringing and the clear sea embraced the island; we were drawn into the narrow streets and lanes of the city.

I chose a rickshaw driver who provided me with sticks of the local weed and took me to an old wooden hotel which had beautiful painted tiles inlaid on the walls and floors. The rent was a dollar a night. The view from my window over the roof tops of Penang was dreamy, and I took the time to just sit there and feel the place vibrate before going out for my evening walk around town. The best, maybe the only way to appreciate a new town is to walk up and down its main and side streets from one end to the other.

A strange omen passed through me that night in Penang. As I was falling into sleep, I saw a huge bat fly over the partition and into my room. It was a great, black, beady-eyed thing, not like the relatively innocuous bats who inhabited our barn back in Vermont but an actually terrifying apparition. I was so stoned that I thought for a moment I might be hallucinating this creature, but shortly it left its perch on the roof beams and swooped down on my face, just grazing my nose as it swung up again. I screamed.

I swore not to fall asleep until I had seen that bat out the window or dead — but somehow, exhaustion crept up into my limbs, starting at the tips of my toes, and I collapsed into deep slumber despite myself. When I woke in the morning, the bat was lying dead on the floor beside my bed, inches from my face, and I had a vague recollection of having killed it with a broom in the night. I swatted it down and pummeled it dead, all while completely asleep. Or at least that's what I *think* happened. Anyway, I wrapped up the corpse and dropped it into the gutter, remembering the times in my childhood when I had walked in my sleep, even devouring whole jars of cookies in my folks' pantry while dead asleep. I

111

wondered what percentage of people I've met and spoken to in my life who were themselves sleeping at the time. And I wondered why this bat had chosen me to do combat with, that is, whose soul inhabited it.

The omen was well taken, though, and I checked out of the hotel that morning and determined to find some quiet place in the countryside in which to wait out my six days in Penang. There was an Indian passenger-and-cargo-ship named *State of Madras* which would sail for Madras in six days, and I managed to buy a second-class ticket (for about ninety dollars) and had only to conserve my cash and lie back in the meantime.

I had learned by this time never to carry more baggage than I could comfortably fit into my knapsack, leaving both hands free to grab onto lifesaving posts as I boarded buses, trains, and boats. So, despite my diminishing resources (about three hundred dollars at the time I entered India), I was as totally free as I could have imagined being. The unhappiness I had met in Hong Kong was all but obliterated from memory by the busy and productive weeks in Thailand. The sun seemed to make my path all the easier and more joyful as the days passed. Deep in poverty, I was learning how to give.

A few visits to Penang's bars and cafés led me to fellow travelers who said the right place to go was a beach about twenty miles around the other side of the island. The place was called Batu Ferringhi and a convenient city bus went there for a nickel. Snaking around the ocean-front highway, a narrow paved ribbon around green cliffs tumbling to the sea and golden beaches stretching out at intervals, I was reminded of coastal Route 1 in California between San Francisco and Big Sur — as it looked and felt before the monstrous swarm of tourist traffic began. Even the sense of stoned, cosmic, hilarious abandon was the same as those early-sixties days in California.

Malaysia would have to be called rich by Asian standards. Fertile and blessed with an ideal climate, it was bursting with food. Singapore and Penang hosted ships of all countries of the world, and their people and cargo. Both cities had some degree of Western style and thinking. Newspapers talked of the Malay standard of living as the highest in southeast Asia, but internal political strife was still trying to shape the control of the area, as it had been since the British granted Malaysia independence fifteen years ago. The majority of the population was Malay but a large minority, perhaps 40 per cent, was Chinese — and these two groups simply never mingled. They might pass each other on the street or ride on the same bus, but they never spoke. Occasional flurries of violence have been going on as long as anyone can remember, but open warfare has never been threatened.

Batu Ferringhi was a stunning beach village separated into distinct Malay and Chinese camps. The Malays lived in wooden shacks with thatched grass roofs, usually very bare and simple inside. The Chinese had neat cottages, much more furnished and swept, in which the walls were often covered with pasted-up calendar pictures from years past. The Malays fished while the Chinese farmed and ran businesses.

There were no hotels in the area, just two restaurant-stores, but it was easy to rent a room in a private house since

113

nobody valued their privacy more than the extra income. In this way, I managed to live in both Malay and Chinese households, finding both good-natured and comfortable.

The beach at Batu Ferringhi looked out over the warm Indian Ocean and the Bay of Bengal, in which I swam every day. I tried to swim a bit further out each time, perhaps believing that with some practice I could eventually swim to Bangladesh or Calcutta. I always emerged oily and with sticky-dry hair, and had to douse myself with buckets of cold clear water behind the grass hut I rented with another American and a Nepalese youth, who had just arrived together from Katmandu. We slept on a wooden floor on thin sleeping bags. Ben was from Philadelphia and enroute to the U.S. He offered me his place in the home of a Nepalese peasant farmer who was an uncle to Ben's companion, Pyaro.

Both Ben and Pyaro were so soft-spoken and genuinely compassionate towards me that I fancied Nepal to be quite a delicate and innocent universe, which it is. We all three of us visited Batu's local Chinese opium den one night, full of expectation of the wonderful high we'd experience. Inside a dark shack by the beach, a half-dozen old Chinese men, their ribs showing through thin bare chests, were lying down on concrete slabs with a rock for a pillow, drawing on long wooden pipes smeared with black, gummy opium. The only light in the room came from the matches and the ghoulish dim glow of the O. The head man informed us in primitive English that it cost one Malay dollar for "six pipes," that is, six refills. We paid and were ordered to lie down. I preferred to smoke sitting up, but the old man croaked at me and gestured to the pallet — "You no sleep, you no smoke." So I "slept," and was properly carried off for my money. But the regular guys there looked so unhealthy, so devastated, that I had a bad feeling about the drug — and shortly thereafter vomited everything inside of me. Gentle Pyaro silently cleaned up the mess, occasionally patting me on the back.

Nights, we smoked in our rooms, peering through graceful palm trees at the glittering ocean across the beach. The house lacked electricity, so we used candlelight, made our own music, and schemed great hash runs between the major capitals of the world. We probably realized that the hash runs were only a fantasy, but all of life was fantastic at the time, so anything seemed real. The house also had a sort of cave man, a great hulking idiot who was the caretaker of the huts; he would cook rice and fish and bring them to us, and he himself ate fish whole, without bothering to remove the bones. He'd laugh and applaud when we sang. The moon grew to full the night before I was to sail to India.

In the morning, we had breakfast at six, and I went out on the road to flag down the bus to Penang City. Ben and Pyaro and the cave man all came out too, and we had a sentimental farewell as I boarded the bus. Then it was straight to the port and a large, gymnasiumlike shed where a mob of passengers, with their baggage, children, old people, trunks, etc., were waiting to be admitted to the M.V. *State of Madras*, which was already four hours behind schedule. When we finally got on the boat, we were exhausted from the impatient pushing of the crowd and the polite interrogation at customs. My new companion, another American, was found with some illegal drugs in his possession, which he sold to the customs officer and left behind.

The *State of Madras* was an uninsured fifty-year-old

115

wooden tanker, which once had been under British management but since 1947 has been run by the government of India. The rumor on the boat was that it was actually condemned and would have to be grounded by law in three years' time. It had rats in the bedrooms and public shower stalls in the corridors, and beautiful brass doorknobs, frosted-glass partitions in the lounge, gracefully carved spiral staircases of dark hardwoods, and old-fashioned tiers of decks — first class, second class, and so on. At the bottom, in Deck class, were nine hundred of the ship's one thousand passengers — just sitting on the deck, on their blankets, surrounded by their bags and families, eating their rice, slurping their sauces, or just lying there groaning, burned by the sun and doused by the rain. We were free to go down there and did, but *they* were prohibited from climbing up.

Once on the Indian boat I was, in some respects, already in India on the high seas. I saw deck upon deck of passengers riding and sleeping open to the weather, shady characters peddling rupees and watches, mothers suckling babies, the dark unknowable souls of all those people I saw. And it left me speechless. I had a sinking sensation down to the pit of my stomach. Somehow, this was the Ultimate Fall, the ultimate return.

"Oh no," I thought, "oh no." I couldn't say more than that. I was under a spell I had anticipated and feared for a long time, but which had also exerted a fatal attraction. Since I must *be* all that I *see*, I was already turning into a victim of material scarcity such as I had never really imagined. Goodby, world! I was being returned to sender (address unknown), material arrived in damaged condition.

116

"This is India," I thought. But what was *really* going on? "What *is* this?" Underneath everything I saw there was something more, some terrifying closeness to sorrow and pain. "This is India but *what is this?*" I heard myself repeating it over and over.

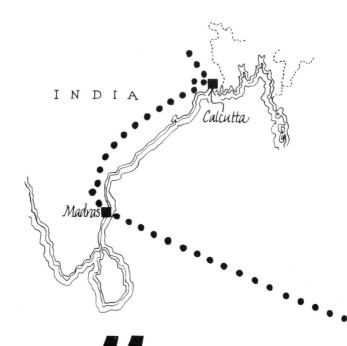

11 IN THE COURSE of these travels, I
spent about seven weeks at sea in various boats during 1972.
Seven weeks to a sailor isn't long, but to me it seemed that an
extraordinarily great part of my time was spent afloat out in
the middle of some comforting void. I realized what a luxury
it was to live as I did. If some of these places seem gruesomely
impoverished to you, remember that if your situation allows
you to move *through* them, your very freedom is compensation enough for the hardships. And even a boat with rats and
poor food and thieving, surly attendants was still a vessel on
the great waters between shores, languages, colors, and
cultures. Such a boat would be peaceful, quiet, slow — but
never boring.

118

The week-long voyage was like a preparation course for India itself. Every day new forms, new ground rules for social conduct in India, became apparent. Compared to the easygoing Thais and Malays, the Indians really create a complex civilization. We were bound up in schedules and forms to fill out. We learned that a torn rupee note, even if perfectly good, will be rejected by all merchants unless you tell them it's all you've got. Waiters bring you food as if you don't deserve it and scream at the top of their lungs if you don't leave a tip. Everybody on board, it seems, is trying to smuggle something into India, as an astonishing variety of things are prohibited or heavily taxed — among them stereos, fountain pens, ball points, watches, dresses, perfume, tobacco, radios — if they are not made in India. These elaborate tariffs obviously protect Indian industry, such as it is.

The captain of the ship took a liking to me, but I hoped I wasn't doing anything to encourage him. He was a great, fat man always dressed in outlandish white shorts and knee socks with a clean white shirt and a proper cap, always sweating and booming orders to his subordinates underfoot. He was imposing and kind of unsavory, and he kept asking me up to his office for a private talk. Finally, I found myself in a situation where it would have been rude, by Indian standards, to refuse, so I followed him up the spiral staircase to his lair. There, he unfolded for me a great treasure chest of forbidden items, including silk saris made in Thailand and a super stereo-cassette system from Japan, bought in Singapore. And, of course, he asked breathlessly whether I'd carry them through customs in Madras for him. (As a tourist I'd get a less thorough examination from the officials.)

I refused to bring the stereo but, not wishing to disappoint him completely, agreed to carry the saris through customs, though I found the idea depressing. He would meet me the evening the ship got in port at an agreed-upon café. Somehow, the experience disappointed me, as I saw the passionate greed in the captain's eyes and realized that in an environment of such deprivation *any* people would act likewise. The stereo system which I found so plastic and offensive was like a pot of gold, the most beautiful thing in the world, to him. Incidentally, the customs man did discover the saris in my pack and immediately accused me of carrying them for one of the ship's crew or officers. And I had to lie, looking him straight in the eye and saying they were gift saris for ladies I would meet in India.

At night the *State of Madras* showed a movie, alternating Hindi films with Hollywood clunkers. None of the rooms inside was big enough to hold the audience, so they showed it on the narrow deck, throwing all the weight of the passengers to one side of the ship. And they'd give you only twenty minutes for dinner before the waiter rushed over, flailing both arms and screaming, "Second sitting! Second sitting!"

But what, in fact, was going on in my mind was like a dream-movie in which I say nothing, judge not, just absorb my surroundings dumbly, contentedly. I counted myself lucky to have any kind of food and shelter and lost myself completely into the *scene*. Riding in second class was like an accommodation which might have been fashionable fifty years earlier; to step downstairs among the deck passengers was like stepping backwards at least two hundred years.

120

Most of the passengers did not feel the same level of distortion of time and space which I felt, since most of them hadn't been hopping through cultures at my pace. But the gut-felt realization of the sweeping differences between life in different lands definitely blew open my mind and, ultimately, contributed some maturity to my way of seeing. What impresses me most is our indefatigable insistence on survival no matter how undesirable our living conditions may become. Men and women are made out of more than flesh alone, of sheer will and *atma* (soul, certainty of fate). And man's real potential is probably infinite. Most of us live, day to day, doing far less than our best, and less than we could do if circumstances demanded.

The world-wide inflation which currently has so many people feeling at the end of their rope is really only a mild flurry of economic instability compared to what already exists in India, where famine is not some terrifying ultimate possibility but a daily reality which people somehow have learned to take for granted. The worst condition that we can imagine our country falling into is still better than the best condition India hopes to create. Yet the people, by and large, believe in a power greater than the world itself, a power which dignifies their suffering, and I felt it too. Expecting nothing, they could be pleased with so little: like the children of the poor. They persist in the belief that having children brings grace in this life, eternal peace in the next, and so keep expanding in population though it's already too crowded to sustain life. Where is the comfort in having a child only to watch it die? In the almost unbearable conviction that God, in His wisdom and mercy, knows and does best for us. It's

121

very hard at first to watch children wasting away — powerless to help and exposed to it every day, you either freak out and have to leave India immediately or get used to it and *seem* not to notice.

Still, the old, agonizing question refuses to go away: are all the people wasting away in India, Africa, even America *supposed* to be doing just that? Couldn't we manage the resources we do have in such a way that nobody had to actually waste away?

On the day before the *State of Madras* was to arrive in port, a certain tension gripped the passengers and crew. Last-minute preparations had to be made; clearly we were about to swim into a storm. Padlocks appeared on trunks and doors and seasoned travelers reminded me to lock the door to my stateroom. The room had only one key, which I shared with my roommates — two middle-aged Malay gentlemen, with whom I had spoken only polite small talk during the voyage. When the two of them went out, they often left me with the key, and if I should go out behind them, they'd have to find me on the ship in order to get back into the room. And vice versa. But on the morning we arrived in Madras, I in my excitement to run out on deck had left the room unlocked. Long before the boat reached shore, barges holding scores of loinclothed porters sailed out to meet us, and this army of mostly naked, sweating men raced aboard and ran amok. Trunks, suitcases, wardrobes were everywhere, officers and crew and passengers mobbing up at the exit doors, and everything fell into a state of utter chaos for several hours. At the height of this madness I saw my Malay roommate running down the corridor toward me, anxiety and fear written across his normally pleasant face. He had returned to the room, found the door open, and discovered his passport and all his money missing.

The ship docked at the steel gray pier in Madras, the steaming city/port of the South, and gateway to Ceylon. The port-side streets were ash black, gravelly, grim; the customhouse an old palatial shed completely desolate within.

My roommate sat forlornly on the edge of his cot, pondering his fate. He wouldn't be allowed to enter India and would have to return to his home in Malaysia on the same boat. I felt guilty and couldn't leave his side. Finally the papers and money were found in the inside wall of the bathroom — as if a thief had hid them there or else their owner had put them there while taking a shower. We were both joyously released.

On the far side of the customs shed, some friends I'd met on the boat were waiting for me; we were to go off together on their motorcycles to find a certain hotel recommended by the captain of the ship. But I wanted my first hours in India to myself — because one's perception of a new place is very different if one has likable companions coming from more or less the same background. Alone, I knew, I would have no distractions to prevent me from absorbing the vibrations of this new land, to which I had so long aspired. With my friends, I'd be involved in a running conversation in colloquial American English, noting this and remarking on that. So, rather than find my friends and explain my sudden need to be alone, I chose to make myself invisible and walked right past them and into the sunshine of Madras. Making yourself invisible is actually easier than it sounds; it's a conscious decision in the mind which, I think, anybody with a strong will could perform. I learned the art of conscious invisibility from a master hypnotist in New York City back in 1971, and it has actually saved my life several times.

Out on the street I was accosted by a lone rickshaw driver whose pedal-driven carriage, topped by a black umbrella, was as threadbare and grimy as its driver. "Where are you coming from?" he asked eagerly. Rows of black crows swarmed to the spot and perched on a long fence behind us. (The crow might be called the official bird of India, for they're everywhere you look.) "Where are you coming from?" is the greeting most Indians will give a foreign traveler, while the Thais and other friendly people in Asia always use the opposite: "Where are you *going?*" It seemed to me that in India one is presumed to be going nowhere; but I had obviously come from another place. I never knew how to answer the question either — was I coming from the last place I'd been, Penang, or from Japan, where I'd just spent two seasons, or from America, which I left behind so long ago? But it didn't matter what I replied, since anything I said would be interesting and acceptable to the questioner. Other questions Indians frequently ask are: "What is your native country?", "What are your qualifications?" (i.e., your educational background), and "What is your spiritual belief?" (i.e., religious affiliation). Indians in general are enthusiastic conversationalists, eager to know everything about you, and unfortunately incapable of understanding when you'd rather be alone, since they are always in a crowd themselves.

The driver, having learned where I came from and where I wanted to go, offered his services for two rupees — less than twenty cents. It was the first moment of my first day in India, and I didn't want to be pedaled about by a servant like some rich tourist. I wanted to walk along slowly, seeing and hearing the life there at its own pace. And I was embarrassed to imagine a fellow human tugging my healthy body through the blazing sun for a few pennies. I politely turned down the offer, saying I'd rather walk, but the driver didn't accept that. He started to walk beside me, chanting over and over, "Sahib, two rupees is all that I ask. Only two rupees, sahib, I do not ask for more. I take you everywhere, your hotel, moneychange man, everywhere. I ask two rupees sahib, two rupees, sahib, no more." Then he'd stop the cab and make a great gesture inviting me to take a seat under the umbrella. The sun bore down mercilessly on our dirt lane, and our steps kicked up an asphyxiating cloud of dust. Again and again I told the driver to go away, but he simply ignored me and kept walking beside me, pulling his bike, demanding my business. Finally I decided to give him two rupees to buy his silence and departure, but realized I had only U.S. dollar traveler's checks. I needed to find a moneychanger right away, and asked the driver where the nearest one was. He pointed to his cab, of course, saying, "I drive you there, only two rupees, etc."

I walked on, now looking for a moneychanger but instead getting deeper and deeper into a neighborhood of stone private houses, their windows shut up against the afternoon sun. There was no life on the street. My emaciated, mustachioed driver, my primeval man, padded barefoot alongside, repeating his simple message, his prayer for my support. I guessed it had been about two miles when I broke

125

under the weight of my knapsack under the sun, and he won. "You win! You win!" I laughed maniacally.

I got into the cab, squeezed in by my knapsack on the seat, and we churned off at a snail's pace, turning off the path and up into a vicinity of narrow streets full of people and shops — women hanging laundry, cows ambling aimlessly, children crawling and playing underfoot, men huddled together in packs exchanging jokes and stories, beggars wailing for the slightest help, cripples and amputees, shit and incense. A mesmerizing scene. And I, in my throne, was the main attraction in the street. Virtually everybody stopped what they were doing to check me out, especially when the driver stopped for a few minutes at the moneychanger's shop. (Almost all shopkeepers in India will also change foreign money, although it's illegal, since Indian rupees are of no value abroad. They can either save the foreign money to eventually leave India on, or trade it back for rupees at a favorable rate. This first moneychanger gave me eleven rupees to a dollar, since I didn't know that the going rate was fourteen. He also had to pay the driver *his* commission for bringing me in.)

We rode away, driving through the circle of gaping onlookers which had formed around the pedicab, and the driver took me to a major boulevard intersection where buses and cars roared past. From there, he said, I could get a taxi or bus to my hotel. I was disappointed because, having finally succumbed and gotten into the rickshaw, I had just become comfortable in it. But I got out and fished out the money in my pocket, finding it to be eleven ten-rupee notes. I offered one to the driver and asked for change. "No change," he said. "That is ten rupees, sahib." Naturally, I told him that the price we'd agreed on was *two* rupees, but he flew into a terrible rage, screaming that I owed him ten rupees, and telling the interested group of onlookers which immediately formed that I had promised him ten rupees and was now trying to cheat him. "Pay him his ten rupees!" a man in the crowd shouted. "This is insane," I thought.

But I stormed around the block, going from shop to shop, and being turned down over and over, until I found a merchant who was willing to change my ten-rupee note; then I returned to the driver, shoved *three* rupees into his hand, and walked off determinedly. It worked. I was free again.

After wrestling with an equally confused motor-cab driver who couldn't find my hotel, I finally arrived at the outer gates of what seemed a handsome villa, surrounded by beds of flowers and climbing vines, a big lawn, and shady fruit trees. Inside the gates, the stone wall cut off a lot of the street noise and dust, and as I approached the verandah of the hotel, I knew I had found an oasis. An older man with healthfully rounded features strolled out in flowing dhoti (a skirt) to greet me and lift the pack from my back. Then we sat down in armchairs by the garden and started to talk. He opened with, "Where are you coming from?", of course, but in soft, dulcet tones. And he was especially keen to know my spiritual mission in India, and promised me that very holy men would cross my path. Well, it felt great, like coming home. Later, he showed me to a clean, simple room with a balcony/patio overlooking the garden, and had one of his servants turn on the water supply, normally used only after

127

nightfall. The rent was ten rupees (eighty cents) a day but the proprietor never asked for it, even when I was checking out. It was almost an *offering*, and the hotel almost a church. The old men always sat outside, smoking *bidis* — harsh little cigars — and discussing the miracles of Mother Kali and the like. Other hotel rooms were available at half the price in the crowded lanes off the public market, but after a day spent in the turmoil of Madras streets, I found the hotel sweet respite and peace. The properietor, so full of generosity and wisdom, assumed a fatherly concern for my welfare. My motorcycle friends from Oregon moved into the room next door to mine, and we all spaced out to the stars every night. I discarded my Western dress and donned the first white *khotas* and dhotis, which I'd wear for all of my time in India and Nepal. I learned to eat food with my hands, and to wipe myself with soap and water after using the toilet. I soon fell into the local pattern of sleeping some hours in the afternoon, when the heat was worst, and walking about in the late hours of the evening, smelling the midnight incense and hearing the hum of people conversing on their porches and roof tops, or down in the street.

I began working on my relations to street people in India, something it would take months to be comfortable with. Basically I had to learn to enjoy the company of a population which would press me for money uninterruptedly — until I ran out of money, when they seemed to intuit my desperation and offered *me* things instead. Beggars, con men, moneychangers, and dope dealers actually dogged my footsteps, and in time I could laugh and banter with most of them, without losing my shirt.

128

Shortly after arriving in Madras, I had filled up my nickel notebook from Thailand, in which I had been keeping a diary and writing letters I never mailed to my friends, and decided to mail the entire book back to Paul Williams, who by this time had returned with Sachiko to New York. So I found the central post office in Madras, entered with the book in my hand, unwrapped it, and went through an entire day's work in order to ship it out. First it had to be examined by several inspectors, who found to their obvious disappointment that it was worthless. (Postal clerks in India examine everything, and even if the contents of a letter or package are valueless, the very stamps on the parcel may exceed the clerk's daily salary. For that reason, it's imperative to wait ·at the post office until you *see* the clerk postmark the stamps; otherwise he might peel them off, throw your letter away, and spend the stamps in a store or restaurant just like cash.)

Despite the worthlessness of my book to the postal bureaucrats, it was absolutely the *most* precious thing to me, and I really felt that by mailing it from Madras — sea mail, sewn up into a cloth package, marked all over with weird rubber stamps — that I was throwing it into the ocean. It might arrive in New York someday, or it might not. Nonetheless, I knew I'd lose it if I carried it around with me in India. The last in a series of clerks I had to visit in order to mail the package wrote on it in crude block letters: BOOK — NO VALUE. And that was the end of my precious child as far as I was concerned. I walked away from the post office grateful to be relieved of my past again. The book arrived six months later in America, at a time when nobody had heard

129

from me in as long a while. I found it impossible to describe India in words while I was there, and even now, two years later, I am sitting in Seattle agonized by doubts that my story really can re-create the place for *your* eyes.

12 LARRY DOLL and Mitchell Danielson left Eugene, Oregon, with the apparently sane idea of buying new Japanese motorcycles tax free in Singapore, driving them through Asia and the Near East to Europe, and selling them there for at least as much as they paid. Thus, they reasoned, they would get a free ride two-thirds of the way around the world. This scheme was reasonable enough, even though they figured only a few months' time to do it in, but like many young American schemers who travel to Asia to take advantage of the low cost of things in one way or other — usually it's dope or art prints and not motorcycles — Larry and Mitchell had overlooked one important consideration: India.

131

They had identical Honda bikes with big 300 cc engines, flashy accessories, carrying racks, chrome everywhere, bright reds and greens — excellent machines which would have drawn admirers even in California, and the likes of which had *never* been seen by anyone in India. From the moment they rolled the bikes off the ship in Madras, they were surrounded by swarms of half-clad humanity utterly awe-struck by the spectacle of these kids and their magnificent wheels. India produces only one kind of car and one motor-cycle — called the Ambassador — and in only one color — black. New or old, these vehicles always look the same — like Chevrolets of the early fifties — and work poorly. Imported cars, like imported anything else, scarcely exist in India, because the tariffs are higher than the cost of the product; these tariffs protect Indian industry, which would quickly collapse if the public were exposed to higher-quality goods.

We shared a big room at a pleasant hotel, surrounded by gardens, in a part of Madras remote from the teeming dirt-lane districts. In the public marketplace, Madras seemed old, heavy, sweet, dangerous, hot, stoned — like a dream of cen-turies ago in the very womb of humanity. Indian con-sciousness is another world from our own; everything that happens to you there seems to be happening in a dream. Just being in India makes a Westerner feel high — that and ex-hausted. India is exhausted too. Government efforts to in-troduce birth control have not succeeded in curtailing the increasing birth rate; already there are 600 million people and not enough food in circulation to go around. Seen from the dirty open window of a third-class passenger train, like a human-cargo freight car creeping along under the sun, the land is barren and dry in most provinces. The crippled and maimed, the limbless and lepers, deformed children — all these and more are everywhere. India is a knockout punch.

Madras was hotter that May than any weather we'd ever known. Numbers of people died of exposure to the sun. The temperature fluctuated from 90° to 130°. To ride unprotected on a motorcycle under such a blazing light was nothing short of insane, yet we did it without stopping to consider; given the poor condition of Indian roads and the scarcity of electric light outside the cities, it would have been impossible to ride at night. We set out for Calcutta, 1,000 miles to the north, expecting to arrive there in five days. Five days later we were scarcely 150 miles out of Madras. The road out of town was filled with people and cows, and the road in the countryside filled with holes. The going got rougher every day. Each time we stopped, a crowd formed around us immediately. They pulled at the motorcycles' accessories; in fact, they pulled at us — our clothing, arms, legs. They stand and gawk at you while you're making a bowel movement. They will ask you for anything without embarrassment, and some of them will steal anything that you don't lock up; consequently, everything of material value, including food supplies in private kitchens, is locked with big brass padlocks sold on the street by emaciated vendors. At times, passengers on trains are locked into their cars — to prevent more frantic people from cramming into the already packed compartments. The windows on trains are usually barred, and wise travelers never go to sleep on a train without first putting their money, passport, and papers into a bag that hangs around their necks. All of this is not to say that the people are dishonest — not any more so than any other kind of people — but they are competing for inadequate material resources in an economy of extreme scarcity. God forgives their being clever thieves, and so do I. But when you are far from home, eating less than you are accustomed to, working harder than you've ever had to, and somebody takes all your money or traveler's checks or your all-important passport — you feel low, you feel scared. Larry and Mitchell had motorcycles to worry about, I had only my feet; their motorcycles were severely damaged by India, and so were my feet.

There was no shortage of gasoline, but it was of lower octane rating than is permitted in the West and Japan. The Hondas were manufactured to use high-test, and their sensitive pistons reacted very badly to the crude fuel. Getting a tire repaired in some medieval stone shed might take all afternoon. Waiting at a train crossing could be an hour or two. Nobody cares but you.

I remember a certain Brahman restaurant in Madras where we went, famished, for a meal in the still of the night. The proprietor spoke Victorian English, as many Indians do who were educated by the British before the Indian independence of 1947. He rapped enthusiastically about the Brahman class, the virtues of vegetarianism, and the price of salvation. Larry asked for a spoon with which to eat his mushy dish of rice and sauces, and the café owner roared with derisive laughter: "Eat it with your hands as we do — see?" I surrendered at once and began shoving the rice in with a cupped right palm and fingertips, stopping now and then to lick off the sauces. "So!" the proprietor approved. "That is correct! This man comes from everywhere."

Or I remember the morning we drove into a swarm of veiled women at dawn. It was on the road in the state just north of Madras, out in the middle of the desert, and the new day's light was just beginning to color the sky. We heard the women before we saw them — they were chanting and making a high-pitched wail. They were walking toward us, their veils and saris floating behind them in the wind, and they seemed like a flock of wild crows moving en masse to the south. Not a single man accompanied these hundreds of women, and we never did learn the purpose of their journey. But the image of them in my mind has never died.

Or the one-legged street urchin who followed me around Madras walking with a stick. I dreaded the clop-clop-clop of his pitiful stick dogging my footsteps, behind my back. I did not turn to look at him, knowing that would make it impossible for me to escape without paying him for his perseverance. Finally, when I sat in a restaurant drinking coffee, he stood beside me, staring into my eyes, saying nothing. He was not more than ten years old. "Do you want something to eat?" He shook his head violently, no. "Something to drink?" No. "What do you want from me?" He spoke: "You are going to picture show?" (He had seen me buy a ticket to a movie theater earlier.) "I come too?" So we watched the cowboy picture together until he curled up, tired and satisfied, and fell asleep in his cushioned first-class seat. I left the theater before the film ended, leaving him to wake up alone.

Or the small town where our motorcycle trip to Calcutta abruptly ended. The bikes were knocking loudly, carrying racks twisted, tires beat, and riders on the verge of a collapse. No gas was available and our rupees were all spent. Nobody in the town could exchange U.S. dollars for rupees and the banks were closed for three days. (Even when they are open, Indian banks are more trouble than they are worth; they also give only half as many rupees as you can get from the street hustlers. Approximately 70 per cent of the cash and goods transactions in India pass through this black market rather than the accountable government bank system.) It seemed we could go no further, so we pulled up the bikes under a spreading palm tree by a high stone wall and sat down in the dust to die.

Moments later, a servant boy appeared from behind the gate in the wall. "My master says do you want some cold beer?" he asked. Cold beer! It seemed at least as attractive as enlightenment. He led us through the gate into what was evidently a mission, with a stone church on the right and gray-white stone tower on the left. Up the spiral steps to the top of the tower we went and walked into the bird's-nest office and home of an elderly Italian architect, named Brother John, who had been in India for thirty years. He was pacing around the room, evidently agitated about something, and while his servant brought us the beer he exploded into a lecture: "What do you mean by this, riding on motorcycles in this sun? Are you crazy? Do you want to die? It is May! We do not go out in the sun in May for more than a few minutes! You crazy, you crazy! You will put the motorcycles on the freight car and send them and yourselves by the train, do you understand?" And so on. We had to let him tell us what to do, since we obviously knew nothing. He produced food, cold drinks, showers, comfortable chairs, reservations on the train, and eventually calmed down and told us the story of his life. He even changed our dollars for rupees at the current black market rate! By the time we left, Brother John had given us everything we lacked and we never had to ride the bikes again — although Larry and Mitchell did drive them to Europe, where they sold them at a loss.

They went to the freight cars to ride with their motorcycles on the train — there being no effective insurance in India for anything you leave unattended — while I wandered around and took a later train for Calcutta. Brother John had strenuously suggested we ride second class, but the price difference was so great that I purchased third-class tickets instead. Nearly everything in India operates on a one-two-three class system, with many subtle distinctions in classes of people ranging from the superwealthy former maharajahs who do not yet pay taxes to the obscenely disadvantaged Untouchables. White foreigners are expected to travel first class, so the presence of an occasional broke American in the third-class rabble is still novel enough to generate some fascination.

Every seat was occupied before I boarded the car, so I found myself standing with many others on the loading platform of the car; the man crammed against me found my presence highly objectionable. "Sahib, you do not belong here! You should be in second class at least! Get off at the next station and have the station master find you a seat in another car!" he shouted. When I tried that, the station master was nowhere to be found and the other passengers in second class had locked themselves in so as not to be disturbed by the anxious masses. I continued riding third class until fatigue and suffocation forced me out at a small town in the

137

middle of the night. There, I ate some *chapatis*, rice, and *dahl* and fell asleep on a wooden bench.

I woke to find an old man dressed in clean white *khota* and dhoti, standing over me, smiling and gazing into my eyes. "So you have come to India at last! I have been waiting for you!" he exclaimed. He seemed ecstatic. He asked many questions about my "philosophy of life," encouraging me to say what he believed — that I had left the gaudy pleasures of a materialistic society in preference for the spiritual uplift of India. That I was not a Christian. That I would not eat meat. All of these things were true to a degree, but my mind was still working to convince myself. Some part of me would have jumped at a McDonald's hamburger or a cold Coke. But the old man was so kind I couldn't disappoint him. He read my palm and seemed to know a lot about me by intuition. "Big name, little money. Soon all the money will be finished. Finished. But you will live to be very old and die a happy man." When the train for Calcutta pulled in, he insisted on riding with me for some hours, although he wasn't going anywhere himself. He made a comfortable seat for me out of sacks and bags on the floor of the car and bought me fruits and drinks at every stop. "This is my friend from America," he announced, "who has come to India to find his guru!" Talk of gurus made me nervous precisely because I had some such idea as well but was guarding it to avoid disappointment if the magic inspiration failed to materialize. Eventually my benefactor got off the train with a tearful farewell, many hugs and kisses. Indian men are not ashamed to kiss each other and often walk hand in hand on the streets. On the other hand, they are extremely reserved with women, especially in public.

138

The people are of course given to a philosophy of non-violence, but the pressures of life are so demanding that they are also highly volatile when in crowds — and more so when it's very hot. Delhi and Calcutta are famous for shockingly violent street demonstrations, especially labor marches, and any train station, post office, or market can explode when the people are pushed too far. I remember once boarding a third-class car and being lucky enough to win a seat — that is, a few inches of hard wooden bench to call my own. I waited patiently for two hours in the unmoving train while the car filled to capacity with people sitting on the floors and hanging from the overhead bunks. At that point, the railroad authorities decided to change the car into a ladies-only compartment — unaccompanied ladies are not considered safe in a car with men other than their husbands or fathers — and a full-scale riot broke out.

All the people in the car were aware that they'd never find space on another car once ousted from this one. The railroad men had to toss them onto the platform, one by one, while one and all resisted with fists, feet, and screams. I spent half the time protecting my head with my arms and the other half fighting officials who were trying to lift me from my seat. Fighting seemed the right and only thing to do under the circumstances. We were valiant, but finally defeated, and had to wait many hours for the next train.

I arrived in Calcutta more tired and dirty than I had ever been in my life. What a strange, dusty energy I found there — both intellectually alert and timelessly slow, furious and inert, charming and alarming. The main pavilion of Howrah Station in Calcutta rivals all the misery movies Hollywood has ever made. Mobbed, mobbed. Hot, hot. There is a woman sleeping on the concrete floor surrounded by five naked children like points on a star of which she is the center; people have tossed a small pile of *paise* coins at her feet, of which she is oblivious but which are, miraculously, safe from thievery. Here are rushing travelers fighting for tickets — city people in India, it seems, cannot wait patiently in a line but will always crowd up to the clerk, waving sweaty rupee notes in their palms and shouting for attention. Young boys are peddling "ice cold soda ice cold" which is invariably as warm as their blood. Great black Gothic arches support the high ceiling of the ancient station, a relic of the days when British construction crews fashioned majestic coliseums in the image and likeness of their fatherland. How grim and chalky these monuments are alongside the splendor of the Taj Mahal! Wailing beggars plead for baksheesh — a gift in the name of God. "Baksheesh! Baksheesh!" they croak, they kneel, they cry. One man vomits on the ground and another man eats it hungrily. I felt a stirring, a swooning. "This is India but *what is this?*"

No taxis were around when I stepped into the blistering sunlight outside the station; a pack of speed-talking hustlers latched on to me immediately and began negotiating the price of a human-drawn rickshaw to the Salvation Army Hotel, my destination. I hadn't the faintest idea where it was but would have walked rather than be pulled by a human mule in that heat; but of course both driver and hustler refused to direct me to the place. They wanted ten rupees from me. I offered and finally paid five rupees. A normal passenger would have paid no more than one rupee (seven or eight cents) for the half-hour ride. I sat in the rickshaw with a giant black umbrella over me as we moved slowly — sometimes slower than a walk — through the incredible dream-streets packed with life and death, mucus and manure. Cars dodged cows everywhere. Great rivers of sweat coursed down the back of my driver. In three months' time I would take such journeys by rickshaw nonchalantly, realizing that the driver was overjoyed to pull me, especially at five times the normal price; but I was bathed in guilt. I felt sorry for everybody, including myself.

But I have learned that how you feel about what you get depends on what you expect. The Salvation Army Hotel in Calcutta, though it might be labeled a pitiful slum dormitory if it were in New York, seemed actually delightful to me. The room rent of a dollar a day included three reasonably filling meals of starch, vegetables, and a little meat, all cooked blandly without a trace of spices or even salt and pepper, in the apparent belief that Europeans (the term includes Americans) could not stand the hot Indian cuisine. The hotel was open to Europeans *only*, in fact, which meant you had only to worry about the servants stealing from you and not the other guests as well. Each guest got a narrow bed with clean sheets in a bare room containing eight or ten beds in a row and a toilet with a cold shower. Hot water was never available in my experience in India and I quickly forgot it existed. The room boy would bring bundles of *ganja* (grass) wrapped in newspaper for four rupees a package. I enjoyed returning to the Salvation Army every night after my hot, hard days tooling around Calcutta, rapping with the fierce Bengali intellectuals, trying to get the American Express clerks to refund my stolen traveler's checks (which disappeared while I was sleeping at the hotel), putting off the chief of police who wanted to hold my hand for hours (I had gone to his office to swear an affidavit about the checks), dodging the perils, exploring the sights, and drinking sweet, cold mango shakes! I visited Calcutta three times over a six-month span and always used the Salvation Army as my home.

The other guests included some of the most intriguing and articulate people I'd ever known, and there were new ones every day. In time Calcutta itself seemed like my own town; I cherished its streets, book shops, familiar aggravations. Though indisputably a disaster area, it is also the intellectual seat of India and the birthplace of the clever Bengali mind. "One Bengali is a poet," they say; "two Bengalis are a political party, and three Bengalis are *two* political parties." A day in Calcutta produced effortless exhaustion, and a stoned evening could be pure bliss.

I entered India with scarcely enough money to live there for a month or two and not enough to get home from there. "Home" to me meant Japan at that time; I knew I could always make a life in Japan and had a recurrent dream (or nightmare) in which I was in San Francisco, Calcutta, or London trying desperately to get back to Japan and getting no sympathy from my friends, who didn't understand my anxiety. After my traveler's checks were replaced, which took several weeks of ponderous Indian bureaucracy, I put some of them in a bank safe-deposit vault which opened not with a key but with a password — "peace." There was enough set aside to get to Singapore at least. While waiting for the checks, though, I had to find a way to live for free — just like everybody else in India.

142

At that point I received a long-awaited letter from a Bengali friend who is now a successful accountant living in Montreal; we had met years earlier in England and he was something of a counselor to me. His family lived a hundred miles west of Calcutta in the village of Suri, West Bangal. They would be very pleased to have me as their guest, Subhas said, and so I was introduced to the Indian household.

At the train station in Suri, I asked the station master for directions to the home of Dr. Sudhansu Panja, Subhas's brother-in-law and the chief man of the family since Subhas's father had died and he and his brother made it to North America. A village boy walked me across the tracks and through the small marketplace to Dr. Panja's house in the center of town, which was tightly locked as the entire family was having its afternoon nap inside. I walked around the village in less than ten minutes, attracting a great deal of attention from the sweet, simple people who had never seen a Western man wearing Indian dress. Then I sat on a stone wall outside Dr. Panja's house and resolved to wait there until he appeared.

The great wooden door creaked open at last and a stout, sleepy-eyed Dr. Panja was before me; his eyes were big, brown, and so kind! We opened his storefront office and sat down to tea, cookies, and cigarettes. I presented my letter of introduction, written in Hindi script, and soon all the women of the household, Subhas's sisters and cousins, were waiting on me and all the men politely calling to make their introductions. I presented gifts of *yukatas* from Japan for the grown-ups, oil pastel coloring crayons for the children, and Japanese cooking utensils for Subhas's old mother, who lived alone in her own house, the widow bereft of husband and sons.

"Now you will stay here," Dr. Panja announced with one eye on the calendar, "some days." I realized it would take "some days" to get into the rhythm of this little town, appreciated the total security of meals and a place to sleep, and at the same time feared for some nameless entrapment in the folds of a society more polite and rigid in its way than Japan's. Americans, all of them, want to know when the show starts and ends, how long they are expected to stay. They want the freedom to leave whenever the mood strikes them — even the freedom to leave their own families and jobs. They also want some privacy. None of these luxuries are available to most Indians, and I simply had to accept the fact that Dr. Panja, and not myself, would determine where I could go and when I could leave. Moreover, he would do so in a spirit of the purest love and elaborate concern for my welfare. What an ungrateful wretch I would be if I were unable to accept this hospitality in the same spirit! But I loved him and the family deeply, and loved watching them at their chores and he at his healing profession. Long hot afternoons passed like slow-motion film. I was not allowed to work, nor even to walk around without an escort; Dr. Panja feared the sun on me. Cooking and serving food was the exclusive province of the women, who did it cheerfully and well; I couldn't get over my indoctrination into women's liberation at the hands of American women, however, and so couldn't graciously accept being served. If I objected that my mountain of rice was far too much to eat (I weighed less than 100 pounds at the time and preferred to eat lightly because of the heat), the entire family would protest and watch me until I ate every grain. They had only one bed and insisted that I use it while they slept on the floor. My indebtedness grew.

In the evenings the family would gather on the roof of the house to take advantage of the cool night air. Since the heat required an afternoon nap, we could stay up very late. The only electricity in the village was at the train station which we could see plainly from the roof. Watching the trains pass through became one of my chief preoccupations; they too were dreams, fantasy ships to the vast desert and the high Himalaya Mountains, not super bullet-trains or even clunky Amtracks, but ancient wooden and iron freight cars to the stars. On trains like that, I would visit fabulous kingdoms! Sikkim, Nepal, Bhutan! More and more, I forgot the days slipping past on the calendar and dreamed my life had jumped into the eighteenth century — that there would always be rice and *dahl* for dinner, and melons and sweet candies for tea time, that there would never be medicine for the villagers' liver ailments and terminal diseases, that there would ever be sympathy and kindness and unspoken understanding of human suffering all around me.

When the morning of my departure dawned, Dr. Panja had already become a father and brother to me, and his sprawling family were mine as well. No real relative of mine had ever spoon-fed me quite so intimately since I was a baby. My mind had slowed to a sharp awareness of mystical reality and my body calmed to a rhythm-of-function in the course of my weeks at Suri. I was rested almost against my own will and had restored myself enough to attack the tumultuous streets of Calcutta once more.

145

As we stood together at the station, Dr. Panja gripped my hand and said that I would surely find what I came to India searching for. "Yes, and I will take it back to America, just as Subhas will bring America back to you," I said. It was a foolish effort to be cheerful and optimistic. "No, Subhas will never come back to India," Dr. Panja said, looking to the ground.

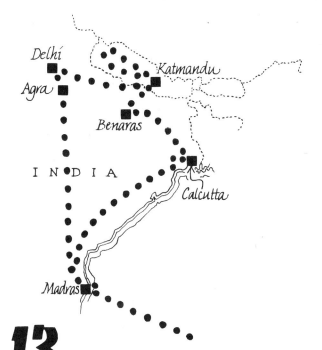

13 WELL, I abandoned all hope of escaping India, which is the only way you can really *see* India. Days passed without incident, weeks and months slipped through my fingers. I met many people, went everywhere on third-class trains, but so much of what transpired is now lost to my memory, like dreams you remember in the morning but have forgotten by the following night. I began to meet young Americans and Europeans who had already been in India for years, some with spiritual masters and others with the Peace Corps, some in search of identities and others buying up lots of shirts and incense to sell in Los Angeles boutiques. Every kind and quality of humanity passed through the jammed streets of India's cities,

147

like a grand epic drama on the state of civilization. Despite the ever-present catastrophes, most of what went on was ethereal, soothing, uplifting. The disasters induced a consciousness of the power of God, and a real fear of His vengeance.

I lived without shelter for a time, just moving across northern India in an arclike northwest direction calculated to land me in New Delhi eventually. Sleeping on trains, benches, and in public parks was common enough and always possible, and sometimes "perfect strangers" took me under their roofs. Outside of major cities, the people were definitely less tense and more generous, even if no more prosperous. I headed up the sacred river Ganges to the ancient city of Banaras, once the most important city on the subcontinent, and still the holy place where millions of Indians go each year to burn their dead and scatter their ashes into the river.

Banaras had been both praised and damned to me by those who'd come from there. As the oldest city in India, it was full of beautiful art treasures and magnificent ashrams dating to the Middle Ages; the sitar factory there has been making the most elegant sitars in the world since 1500; the river itself, and the funeral pyres on its banks, is an unforgettable spectacle. But the people were said to be "incredibly aggressive." The government of India ran a tourist hotel in Banaras, which was the only refuge from the frantic energy of the town.

But when I'd fought my way through an army of rickshaw drivers, selecting one and agreeing on the price, my driver refused to take me to the Government Tourist Hotel.

148

He kept arguing that he knew a better hotel and took me to half-a-dozen of them — expecting, of course, some payment from the hotel manager if he could persuade me to take a room. I sat in the sunshine getting progressively more angry, and demanding to be taken to my hotel. Then he began taking me to more hotels, saying, "This *is* the government hotel," when it obviously wasn't. Finally, I seized my black umbrella and began beating the fellow over the head and shoulders, and it worked! I screamed, he ran, we got to the hotel, he demanded three times the agreed payment, etc. I took a room and lay down on the bed shaking with rage and humiliation. I hadn't been physically violent since I was twelve years old.

On the streets of the holy city, more of the same. Shopkeepers grab you as you pass, trying to sell you their wares; moneychangers on every corner whisper their latest quotations; beggars plead. I went to the *sitaram* with two friends from the hotel, and we were treated to a private concert by the master, who gave me a letter to deliver in the United States. We discovered an ice cream factory where you could get such things as mango and papaya ice cream cones, scooped by a sweet ten-year-old girl whose father owned the place, in a dark cool tingling environment. We separated, and I went off alone to visit the riverside, where the funeral services are going on twenty-four hours a day. For most Hindus, to be burned on the Ganges at Banaras is the cherished and wished-for perfect culmination to their lives.

Unfortunately, I attracted a kid of about sixteen years who wanted to sell me something — anything — and walked beside me down to the river. He offered watches, hashish,

149

Chinese girl; I kept telling him to go away as I was walking to the holy place. "But how can you not want *anything*?" he persisted. "I want nothing! Now go away! I don't like you!" I shouted, stopping in my tracks. He was undaunted, began flailing his arms. "Why have you come here if you don't like Indian people?" he accused. "I like Indian people, I don't like YOU!" I was finished. The river loomed ahead, cloaked in the thick white smoke of burning flesh and incense. He turned and ran.

I worried that the mission I had begun for peace was turning to such an ugly and angry mood.

The whole scene at the funeral pyres reminded me of a public festival for some reason — all the people dancing and swaying, families gathered together, the enormous spectacle of an important man's tall pyre shooting up into flames. There was none of the gloomy politeness of Western-style funerals. Although the mourners were grieving, the ritual was overwhelming everything else and most of the people, I think, felt real joy at committing their departed to his new life in the proper and most sacred way. Death is only the beginning for a Hindu believer.

But it can be the end for his widow. Hindu wives are still forbidden to remarry, no matter how young they might be when their husbands die, and as widows many will not be supported by their original families. The plight of the widow is so lonely and poor that even now some resort to the ancient practice of *sati*, in which they hurl themselves on their husband's funeral pyre and go out of this life by his side. That way lies salvation.

I was awe-struck by the place but left there after several

150

hours feeling somehow uplifted and secure. Back through the winding narrow lanes, passing saffron-robed bodies being wheeled down to the Ganges, I dodged peddlers and made it safely back to my room, there to meditate the hot afternoon hours away on a contemplation of the blank wall.

When it was time to get on towards New Delhi, I had the bad luck to board a train on which every car seemed full to bursting. It creaked along through the morning, I standing up on the loading platform, jammed between other people's shoulders and holding my knapsack tightly between my knees in a pool of water and sludge. When the train made one of its typical interminable stops (an hour or two) at some small station, I determined to find a new car and went walking up and down the length of the train. Incredibly, I spotted a third-class car in which nobody was standing and there were even a few vacant seats. Tightening my knapsack against my back, I began to board it.

A terrific force, like some reverse vacuum, pulled me off the boarding steps backwards, and I felt myself falling to the pavement below. I hit the concrete with a thud and clunked my head. When I opened my eyes and looked up, I saw a fat Northern Railway conductor looming over me; he had obviously pulled me off the train by my knapsack. He was booming something about the car I had been attempting to board; apparently the seats were reserved and it was his job to protect them against the likes of me.

But my reaction was anger, almost homicidal blind rage, and I scrambled to my feet and without a word began pounding my fists into this huge conductor's ample belly. A crowd formed around us as I punched him back against the train, now issuing bloodcurdling screams. None of the men in the crowd, including the astonished conductor, made a move against me. They all gaped at my behavior in total, motionless amazement. I doubt that I hurt the conductor at all, actually, but when I stormed off and out of the station, I had to sit under a tree and reconsider everything about my pilgrimage to India.

Although the pressures of life in India for my first couple of months may have been severe — nobody likes being thrown to a concrete pavement when they haven't intentionally done anything to deserve it — still I couldn't find any excuse for the ferocious temper I had suddenly acquired. The fact that others around me were sometimes more violent than I wasn't pardon enough. If I needed to use my fists to survive in India, I thought, I should leave immediately. The issue of violence was a moral consideration to me. I knew, somewhere deep inside of me, that violence is never a creative force.

Obviously, I had to learn, and did learn, how to live in India without losing my calm center. But that followed. My immediate reaction, following the punch-out, was to change trains and, even though I'd bought a ticket to New Delhi, get and ride the "express" train north to Nepal. Fortunately, I had acquired a Nepalese visa back in Calcutta, so I simply reversed my path and headed for the hills, so to speak, in the spirit of fleeing India in real concern for my sanity.

The trip to the border of Nepal took two days, as I recall, but they passed easily in the shadow of the Himalayas in my horizon and in the company of a dozen or more European freaks who got on the train in pairs and threes as we approached the border. Finally, half the car in which I was riding was taken by young people from the Western hemisphere, most in stages of physical decline. We were the latest crop of Indian-pilgrimage refugees to arrive in Katmandu.

By the time we reached Birganj, the first town in Nepal, the train was almost empty, a refreshing departure from the usual. The air was cool and clean. All the passengers climbed into pedal rickshaws and crossed the tiny border shack, where formalities were minimal. And a hotel, just one, was provided where you slept twenty-four beds to a room for about a quarter, and the café served egg curry and beer. Birganj was not much of a town, but it was distinctly different from any town in India. It was light, airy, easy, friendly. The anxiety was gone, although the poverty was equally dire. And everybody, from eight-year-old urchins underfoot to old men with white beards, was smoking hashish in stone chillums and in devastating amounts.

But Nepal was more than a stoned paradise for idle hippies. You actually caught the sense of something supernatural in the air. Scholars and saints, mountain climbers and mystics and Tibetans all converged there, and the energy level was buzzing. Nepal, in 1972, was still a place where you could let your mind go free without fear. The Nepalese character was stunningly different from the Indian one. While the Indians mill and wail and struggle, the Nepalese sit quietly and smile. They are tolerant almost beyond belief. They are, to varying degrees, innocent. Western corruptions have already appeared in Katmandu, of course, and the street hustlers there are afflicted with the same lust for stereos and

153

sleeping bags that drives the black market in Delhi. But, by and large, modern inventions and economics haven't reached Nepal. A rare place.

There's a torturous bus ride from Birganj up to Katmandu, cradled at forty-five hundred feet in a Himalayan notch. The bus has to climb up to fourteen thousand feet or so before it dips back down into the Katmandu Valley, with its terraced-step rice fields and tropical vegetation. The bus leaves Birganj around seven A.M. and arrives in Katmandu at nightfall — that is, if nothing goes wrong with the engine, the weather, or the narrow, perilous road. The road is closed in the rainy season for months at a time, but a small, bumpy airplane flies between the capital and the Indian border once daily.

When we finally entered the gates of Katmandu, I was exhausted and interested primarily in getting settled for the night. But the sweet vibrations, the roof tops and street-side shrines, the smiling faces of Katmandu enchanted me, and I spent the better part of the evening walking around dirt lanes, getting acquainted. Here I found all the people I'd met in passing in Thailand, Hong Kong, Malaysia, and India; here they lived in inexpensive luxury and near-total inertia. Miniature Tibetan people strolled through the central square, their robes flowing and bells tinkling gently. Merchants sat on wooden boxes, surrounded by their wares, happy to buy and sell but slow, considerate, contemplative, never aggressive. On the edge of town, in full view of most of the open plazas of Katmandu, stood the Monkey Temple, thousands of stone steps up a steep green hill, inhabited by an army of scampering cute monkeys, capped by a pointed

154

four-sided tower on each face of which a huge, blue, un-blinking eye was painted. Thus God in his temple saw everything we did below.

The most famous café in Katmandu at the time was Aunt Jane's Place on Dharma Lane, which was reputed to be owned by an American diplomat's wife and to serve real American hamburgers, BLTs, and so on, and even real chocolate cake and apple pie! And so it did, but despite my best efforts I couldn't find the place this first night I went out looking for it. But I found better places by far, like the Tea Room where ten-year-old Nepalese boys raced around bringing pancakes, eggs, *lassis*, and tea to customers who sat at an old wooden table on a long bench. And the temple itself, accessible via a long, swaying footbridge of planks and rope over the river; it fairly glowed in the moonlight. And the Matchbox Lodge, where I lived for more than a month with the warmest, most carefree group of down-and-out poets, painters, musicians, backpackers, weavers, chefs, soul searchers and path followers I could have hoped for.

We ate together every night at the same small cafe-cum-hashish shop, where a back room (actually behind a long black curtain) with plank table for ten was reserved for us. Some nights, we'd follow dinner with visits to other small joints, finding in each a scene to fall into if we liked. The characters of the people I met were unusually strong, unique, memorable in some way. Wealthy dope dealers from L.A. chatting with actual *saddhus* smelly from caves; daft old lady with dark glasses and long cigarette; stoned Boston coed; aspiring saints. The Matchbox was managed by young boys who brought the hotel rent to older black market operators;

155

but if you couldn't pay your rent — and there was always somebody who couldn't — you just threw up your hands, saying, "Money finished!" and the boys would shrug and say, "Later." There was virtually no anxiety in Katmandu of the kind that we associate with more prosperous cities.

When the money *was* quite finished, I made my way to the home of Pyaro's uncle, who lived a few miles north of Katmandu and farmed, as best he could, to support his house, wife, and four children. Pyaro had given me the uncle's address (just "Swayambu Choagdol Hill") back on the beach at Batu Ferringhi, saying his family would take care of me when I was in need. I went to the right general vicinity and began asking for the house of Shyam Kaji, and shortly found myself in the yard of a great two-story mud-brick hut.

Shyam was young, perhaps thirty, but in that part of Nepal men are considered lucky to live past forty. His wiry frame testified to his life of eating rice and working hard. But he grinned broadly, showing his missing front teeth and the three solitary hairs gracefully growing from his chin. His face was rough, worried, wrinkled — yet it somehow showed his honesty and good nature. Delighted to have news of Ben and Pyaro, he had his wife prepare a room for me, throw a mattress on the floor, and I was instantaneously absorbed into the family, even to sitting with them morning and evening as we devoured rice and sauces with our fingers.

Wanting to make a gift to this family for its hospitality, but having no actual cash, I remembered a long-ignored electric razor I'd received from Hitachi Corporation in Tokyo, as a complimentary sample of the product I was endorsing. It was a bulletlike steel cylinder with a single rotary blade on the top, which snapped with a reassuring click into a green plastic case, ran on one flashlight battery for six months, and marketed for about twenty dollars but looked like a million. When I handed Kaji this shiny rocket-ship of a razor, his eyes brightened like Christmas bulbs; how much was it worth on the market, he wanted to know. I'd once been offered two hundred Indian rupees (more valuable than Nepalese rupees) for the thing. Kaji was ecstatic! He could get enough out of it to rebuild his house. I suggested he try shaving with it once before selling it, but the idea of using the razor just made him laugh with embarrassment and he was far too much in awe of it to press it to his face. I gave his wife my made-in-Japan plastic sewing kit, with a dozen colored spools of thread and as many needles and pins, and a tiny pair of blunt scissors. Her equipment to date had been just a spool each of black and white threads, and one fat needle. I was delighted to find that the remnants forgotten in the bottom of my knapsack, none of them rare or particularly expensive where I came from, were treasured possessions to the people I would meet. Thereafter I made a policy of giving something from my knapsack — a ball-point pen, a shirt, a book — to everyone who gave me shelter, until finally the knapsack was empty and I gave *it* to a peasant who used it to carry vegetables from the fields. And I was agreeably reduced to a green cloth carrying bag, with my U.S. passport my only valuable possession. I never considered getting rid of *that*.

Now in all my wanderings in India and Nepal, I had yet to meet the imagined seer who could help me overcome whatever it was in me that kept me from being happy, calm, peaceful. No matter how lucky my life might have seemed to

157

others, no matter how much or how little success my projects enjoyed, "I" was always forced to move on unsatisfied — that is, my consciousness of myself always interfered with the bliss I hoped to attain. The two things I knew could *obliterate* me were intense sexual experience and real religious experience. But the God I met on my way was not living exclusively in the body of any man or woman, teacher, *saddhu* or guru; not any more than He was living in me. But I knew that the object of my journey was to meet with God, so the goal was also to find myself by losing myself, to reshape and reincarnate myself into a new personality, more patient and tender than the last.

And with all *that* kind of stuff in mind, I started walking. And, walking along on the dusty path out of Katmandu and toward the high Himalayas and Tibet, utterly without supplies or money, without even shoes, and determined to walk until I found It, I was higher than a kite. My situation had become so extraordinary in terms of my past experience that I could only laugh at the delicious insecurity and complete freedom I was feeling. The way goes, snakelike and steep, clear to the roof of the world.

I am standing

Still and flying

I am struggling up a rocky staircase to the merciless sun, surrounded by thick walls of sheer gray stone, dark green forests, tumbling waterfalls of silver-cool water from the source, the peaks of high snow-dressed Goliaths on the horizon.

On the first day, I lost my hashish in a small village at the bottom of a particularly difficult climb. I'd absent-mindedly left it behind on the table of an outdoor café where I'd had tea. The thought of picking my way down the mountain and having to scale it a second time was so wearying to me that I kissed the hash good-by, figuring that on *this* trip it would only slow me down.

As the day neared its end, I found myself on the edge of a high bluff overlooking a timeless uncivilized-but-sanctified valley, a small hut to my left apparently put there for the crew of men who were working on a bridge nearby. Two of the men came out to greet me and without hesitation invited me to spend the night with them in the shack. They cooked up some rice and eggs and brewed tea. We talked by candlelight but their questions were simple and not philosophical. Incredibly, I found it just that easy to get housing and food every night of my journey, for I was never turned away from any door. In the really remote areas near Lake Gosainkund, bordering Tibet, the villages were so far apart and so tiny that I frequently placed my survival on the doorstep of whichever place I'd reached that day. People were so universally friendly that I never had to consider the danger of starvation if even one fellow human being was nearby. In some ways, my life was never more elegant. My steps took me around fabulous bends in the road and in my mind. Bit by bit, everything from before fell off my back and tumbled to the foot of the mountains, there to be washed away by the rivers. I climbed into the clouds, three weeks on the calendar but an eternal passing to me.

I stayed several nights in a village where the local general merchant gave me a room which had three walls and was open on the fourth side to the main path of the town. There, I washed all my clothes in the river and got rather badly bitten by slimy leeches which cling to the skin, sucking blood, until they are pulled off by hand, and then leave sores which don't clot for three days. So, with bleeding feet, I was forced to rest up a few days and eventually was taken to a supposedly crazy old man who lived outside the local temple, a hut in the jungle. While the priest stayed inside, observing the proper ritual, this ancient ragman sat perched on the wooden platform by the door, chuckling to himself and smoking *ganja* provided by neighbors who, it was clear, saw he possessed some spiritual power. I stayed up one whole night with him, under a full moon, smoking and enjoying a crystal clear telepathic relationship with him. He was a clever old con man, someone I could really admire, who laughed at the utter absurdity of the world's work.

A few thousand feet up, in the village of Manigoan (pronounced "money-gone"), I even met a guy who had some use for the half-dozen heavy books in English which had been weighing me down. A young, well-tailored man, Raj Lal had studied English in Katmandu and was proud of having memorized one of the finest poems in English, he said:

> What is this life, if,
> Filled with care,
> We have no time to
> Stand and stare?

That gave me something to think about, and while I was thinking Raj Lal came up with this: "How I would love to go to New York where they have *everything!*" I was astonished and, pointing to the huge mountain directly in our view, said, "But what about *that?*" "*That!*" he replied "is *nothing.*" He meant, literally, that there were no buildings, no taxis, no books in Manigoan, Nepal — nothing. To me, it was the sweetest nothing I'd ever seen, to Raj Lal, just a bore. Well, even in cloud-cloaked Himalayan wilderness, somebody thinks the grass is greener in New York. Ain't life grand?

Raj Lal's poem came back to me several days later, when I reached the end of my trail at Lake Gosainkund, where the Indian pilgrims go every August to bathe but which was completely without people or food at the time I visited. I actually sat on a rock and puzzled how long I could continue without rice, wondered whether some higher power might not support me even in the absence of all food and drink. But I didn't believe deeply enough to try it. I knew I had to turn back.

> What is this life, if,
> Filled with care,
> We have no time to
> Stand and stare?

The words poured through me like a melody, and I stood up stark naked on that lakeside cliff and trained my eyes on the horizon. The clouds passed swiftly, racing for the edge of the world, and slowly the ravine beneath me cleared up. I saw a snaking river deep below. Then the local mists rose and the distant clouds just *parted.*

Revealing Sagarmatha, also called Mount Everest, the highest point in the world.

This vision lasted ten minutes or more before the moisture

only the kind faces of strangers who'd never read my books nor heard the whispers of my notoriety. I was released from my past, something most people never achieve, but although my own efforts had helped, it was still through the intervention of some higher power that I was sprung. Time had conveniently chosen to forget me, and I knew I could return home without having to face up to my misdeeds or resume my unhappy romances. I have never since breathed the word "love" without remembering that high place far away, because love, for me, became something greater than a personal attachment to somebody.

I arrived back in Katmandu on a dusty Fourth of July, and some Americans I met outside a brass-pot shop told me that the U.S. Embassy was having a party on its palatial grounds. One's passport was one's ticket, but many Europeans managed to talk their way through the gates and shy Nepalis hung out along the fence, peering in at the strange spectacle. Little blond-haired children hopped along in burlap sacks to win Kewpie dolls. Hot dogs with mustard stripes and freezing cold Miller's beer had been flown in special from San Francisco. A public-address system played the latest Carly Simon hit, "You Want to Marry Me," and the Doors' "Light My Fire," as interpreted by José Feliciano. Splendid waste was everywhere, and the most amazing thing of all — amazing, at least, to the Nepalis and to *me* — was the egg-toss. Hundreds of eggs were flying through the air, each team trying to catch as many as possible before they broke. Most *did* break, of course, and all the American Embassy folks burst into hysterical laughter every time an egg smeared somebody's face or went running down someone's leg.

164

Where I'd just come from a single egg a day could stand between living and dying. The humor of the game was lost on me. I just kept wondering whether Raj Lal would still want to go to New York if he'd seen the American Embassy July Fourth picnic. Probably. Sigh.

Grim as it was, the picnic scene didn't give me second thoughts about returning. I was going home for sure. Went over to the American Express office and got my mail, finding a small fortune ($550) in international checks which I was in no way expecting. It seems I had written a month and a half earlier to a friend in California who became so concerned about the conditions I described at Shyam Kaji's house that she sent money and sent my letter on to other friends. My cover was blown. There were checks from San Francisco; Aspen, Colorado; Vermont; Boston. Clearly my friends were buying me a ticket. Home.

Strolled down through the town, past the tea shops, craft centers, and shrines, through the pigsty by the river and out to the rice field on which the Matchbox Lodge was built. After paying up my back rent to the delighted hotel boys, I found a nice rope cot, threw my stuff on it, and took all ten residents out to the Hotel Crystal, Katmandu's finest, where a dinner of steak and potatoes imported from Thailand ran about one dollar. We had champagne too. In fact, we ate and drank all night, on about as much as a family of four would spend on lean pickings at a Denny's.

I procrastinated for several weeks before leaving Katmandu. The company was so pleasant and I enjoyed the luxurious feeling of being able to gratify all my material desires. I bought a gold silk shirt and an umbrella and felt, like Little

Black Sambo, that I was the grandest boy in the jungle. It was almost as if, having reached the most poverty-stricken level of my life, I was now turned around and heading squarely back into the world of people and things. It goes in spells with me. I discovered the headiest delight in the smallest comforts — I saved rubber bands and plastic baggies because they seemed so valuable to me. And to eat a doughnut or even an icky soyburger was pure joy. Coffee; fresh fruits; shoes. How you feel about what you get depends on what you expect. My days and nights were full of pure happiness and peace. From that time even to now, I discovered the power of ordering my own affairs in something resembling control of my own destiny. I had, simply, grown up, at twenty-six. It was time.

I met an American girl outside the post office one day after I'd overstayed in Katmandu so long that the road was washed out and buses couldn't leave the city. The rainy season had begun. She was a real saint who had been living with Tibetans for the past two years, and who had just come through an unhappy love affair. We started talking, her long brown hair blowing in the wind and rain, and finally she gave me a silver toe-ring with three silver beads tinkling on the end of a chain. Such a ring would only be worn by a lady, she said, but I was to give it to the lady. I treated it as a rare treasure from the East, carrying with it certain vibrations of Tibet, and as a ticket to ride. I flew down to the Indian border on a pouring wet afternoon in August, feeling the toe-ring on my foot through my sock.

In India this second trip, there were no outbursts of temper comparable to the earlier ones, even though Delhi was absolutely the most troubled place in India that I experienced. Once, when suffering from some staph infections in my face, I screamed at a pharmacist who refused to sell me aspirin for no apparent reason; but the screaming was just a physical release of pain and gave me no conscience qualms later.

I met an angelic Swiss teen-ager named Phillippe, head full of curly yellow hair, wearing native dress and eagerly searching for his ashram; and together we went to the Taj Mahal in Agra for three days, returning to it each morning for fresh inspiration. For all the tragic deprivation in India, the Taj Mahal may be the most awesomely rich structure in the world. The approach to it is through a long, green avenue where cars and rickshaws are prohibited, the grounds are perfectly kept, and the shrubbery is consciously landscaped to prevent you from seeing the actual building until you pass through the portals and find it dazzling before you in the distance beyond a vast plaza and pool. *"Oh! C'est beau!"* said Phillippe.

It is a jewel — perhaps the biggest jewel in the world. It positively gleams by sunlight and glows by moonlight. On full-moon nights, the Taj is kept open all night and thousands come to admire its otherworldly light. It is the grandest single *object* I have ever seen. And it reminded me of a time when India was the richest land of all; Columbus sailed from Spain in search of it.

Down in Delhi, though, circumstances took a turn for the worse in a fashion that gave me enough momentum to leave India. The city was inhumanly crowded and traffic choked; for the first three days I had to sleep on the floor of Mrs.

167

Kolikos's hotel, waiting for someone to vacate a bed. Prices for everything were uncommonly high by Indian standards, and an ongoing Twenty-fifth Anniversary of Indian Independence celebration provided the framework for torchlight parades and patriotic fervor in the streets, which were risky after dark. A few modern skyscrapers had been constructed and filled with ludicrously underworked bureaucrats. Delhi's street repair crews actually use two men on each shovel — one to push it in the dirt, the other to lift it up out of the ground using a rope tied to the shovel's end. Here, the government of India resides and declines.

Mrs. Kolikos's hotel was full of beds, cots, floor mats, clothes, and people, eight or ten to a room. "Ma" Kolikos herself was a portly Anglo-Indian woman, proud of the English blood in her and a fervent Catholic. She actually pontificated about virtue and Christ as she took in money. She scooted troublemakers out of the place with a broom, and ruled with an iron hand, or thought she did. All the guests did all the prohibited things (such as smoking hash) behind Ma's back. Airless and tight, the rooms were breeding grounds for communal infections; and the plumbing so seldom worked that it was impossible to keep open wounds clean. But the camaraderie among the inmates was superb, and Mrs. K.'s place, as the only hotel in its price range in New Delhi, served as a kind of communications center for Western wanderers passing through the capital. Some, like me, were there only to get visas and other official documents; some had been there for months and actually chose to live in Delhi; and a few were lifers.

But the environment had so many pitfalls that only a

168

handful of very strong individuals could make a life worth living in the city; the others came down with horrible and even fatal diseases, or simply wasted away on too little food and too much opium, or lost their minds completely. There was a tall, blond-haired guy from California who used to work Connaught Place, the main business circle in New Delhi, nearly naked, utterly crazy, begging for *paise* from his fellow Americans. The story was told that he'd flown directly into Delhi from New York City and had all his belongings stolen immediately; thereafter, he went crazy. One night he tried to sleep in Mrs. Kolikos's place, having no other, but made such a commotion with his begging, wailing, and banging on doors that Mrs. K. called the police, who took a couple of hours in getting over, then finally arrested Mrs. Kolikos instead of the crazy man! She was hysterical and tried to beat up the cop, while all the hotel guests were beside themselves with laughter.

There was a couple from L.A. in my room, Kurt and Janet, who'd been traveling together for several years; this was their second trip to India, their sixth month in New Delhi. They'd been broke for some time, waiting for payment on some stuff they shipped to California, and were running up a bill on the reluctant Ma, who watched their comings and goings closely. Janet had a ring through her pierced nose, Kurt a great mop of curly hair topping an emaciated frame. Somehow they scraped up enough to stay in opium, which in turn killed their appetites, but I started buying them dinner in restaurants every night and eventually succeeded in reviving their taste buds. When I left Delhi, I felt compelled to make some arrangement for their eating in my absence, so left the responsibility to a trustworthy former Peace Corps guy. Since they would never ask, he was to invite them to join him in curry and cakes. They were worth saving.

And there were masters too. I remember a thirty-five-year-old American man, black bearded with gleaming brown eyes, who knew Delhi as his soul and took me to a night meeting with his teacher in an abandoned shed behind some kind of warehouse. We played the flute and smoked and brewed tea all night while the old man chewed happily on nuts and put forth — well, a beam.

Amid all this I felt like a happy observer, not even despairing in the face of the grim famine and illness, not even believing that miracles I saw were unusual in any way. Contrary to the mythology built up around it, I found India no more holy a place than any other, because the essence of our sanctity is not in our geography but in our faith. I could not be persuaded that God is kind after looking at dying in India. But the world *is* as we see it, and I finally accepted Delhi on its own terms.

For three weeks, I had been building some staph infections in my face which resisted all the treatment available to me in the city. As the infections grew, they began to press on sensitive nerve endings in my jaw and teeth, causing the highest degree of physical pain I've ever experienced. Aspirin was effective against the pain but hard to come by and only available in tablets one-third the strength of U.S. aspirin. Penicillin was impossible to find. I was taken to a homeopathic physician who had a small office behind an auto repair shop. His kind, strong presence alone made me feel better, but his homeopathic remedies, herbs and natural extracts dosed into little white sugar pills worked slowly. He did, however, bandage my face expertly, warning me to "keep it clean and keep it covered."

So I left the greasy shop a mummy, relieved to have hope of conquering my poisonous sores at last. But the infections did not drain for two weeks, while it got harder, and finally impossible, to open my mouth to eat. And one day, instead of changing my bandages in my room, I went to a mirror and stripped my face to reveal — what? Some hideous stranger, whose ribs showed through his chest and whose face was hard to bear.

I realized that being nutritiously and contentedly fed, reasonably well clothed, and in comfortably good health was a prerequisite to any further spiritual expansion I intended to do. I was truly thinking like an Indian at last. I resolved to get what I needed to survive, having seen myself dying. A face, even if it isn't beautiful, is *your own*. To have mine so disfigured disturbed some essential self-preserving instinct in me which leapt into action. I made reservations for a sleeping rack on a three-day train route to Madras, where the British-Indian vessel *Rajula* would sail to Malaysia the week following. It takes many hours of waiting around government buildings to secure a train reservation, but I had learned some patience by then, and it was preferable to riding on the floor. I spread out my blanket on the wooden plank, and actually found the train ride easy and relaxing. The infections started draining and healing the first night out of Delhi. The other passengers brought me fruit and blankets.

Off the train in Madras, I walked through the market in

171

the cool, golden sunshine of autumn. I unbandaged my face to give it the benefit of the fresh air. A very old and very strange beggar woman in a bright yellow skirt covered with bells approached me, shaking her bowl in which she kept her day's alms. She was apparently a member of a group of lepers who were wandering in the square, jumping and dancing, their faces painted grotesque colors. She came close to me, looked at me with demented eyes, laughed and gurgled and reached out to touch my sores with her filthy hand.

I felt no anger, no fear. But I pushed her away from me, which knocked her to the ground. Her begging bowl went tumbling down the street, all her coins rolled away. A great crowd formed and, as I started weeping with guilt and with shame, the other people started laughing and pointing to her and grabbing her coins. I walked away from her lying in the dusty street surrounded by jeering onlookers. When I turned around, I saw she had gotten up and run off.

Madras seemed innocent and slow paced after the ruinous streets of Delhi. The old hotel master of the garden villa where I'd spent my first days in India came out to greet me as I approached. "Did you find India?" he asked. "Yes," I replied. "Now go home and have children," he advised.

"There is an analogy of two people walking barefoot along a very rough road, and one thought it would be very good to cover the whole road with leather so it would be very soft, but the other one, who was wiser, said, 'No, I think if we covered our feet with leather that would be the same.' So that is patience, which is not being distrustful, but is a matter of not expecting anything and not trying to change the situation outside oneself. And that is the only way to create peace in the world."

—CHOGYAM TRUNGPA, from *Meditation in Action*.

15

THE *Rajula* crept out of its berth in Madras ever so slowly, leaving the black, sweating mainland behind in a fine mist. It was September, beginning of the "good season" in India as elsewhere, with cool temperatures and golden sunlight. I'd arrived in spring, left in fall, somehow spent a half year in between which felt like a lifetime. I weighed in at 115, weighed out at 90. Left those 25 pounds up and down the path. I felt superbly satisfied with my visit, but still couldn't pin down just what the hell happened to me while I was there. None of it seemed remarkable except in retrospect, but somehow my attitude toward living had changed dramatically. I was hungry for life, hungry for experience; I was living with enthusiasm and eagerness again. The prospect of a good meal would make me unquenchably cheerful, and I never wanted anything more than what I got. All the sights, sounds, colors of the world delighted me. Somehow I knew that where I was going everything was going to seem very easy for a while, and I acquired a certain instant-wiseman glow which I had myself observed on people just coming out of India when I met them in Bangkok or Singapore. Nothing seemed to faze these people; they even attracted followers without seeming to want them. Part of their magnetism lay in their brightness, which one assumed came from the sacred visions they'd had in India, but which actually came from their having survived and finding themselves on Easy Street.

Survival seemed good to me, whereas earlier it had been of doubtful value. I became more concerned with taking care of my health, eating well, and keeping apart from the more insidious drugs and gathering places. I met an ex-Harvard University professor named Carl on the *Rajula*, and since he was also headed for Japan, we decided to go together. Carl

174

was one of a select handful of middle-aged American men who one day up and quit job, leave wife and car payments, make some arrangement for a small monthly check to be forwarded, and travel to distant islands looking for nothing at all. They have a reassuring, mature, matter-of-fact attitude about it all which I appreciated. We picked up a third guy, a young, optimistic Washingtonian named Buck, when we changed ships in Singapore and boarded a Chinese boat for Hong Kong. Buck dressed, looked, and acted like a cowboy and was in the business of selling Indonesian native blankets on the streets of Japan. He was carrying two trunks of these blankets around with him.

So Carl, Buck, and I formed a threesome in Hong Kong, like sailors on the loose, taking ferries all around and sharing a cubicle at the Wing On Travel Service. When our investigations turned up only one ship leaving for Japan, an East German freighter carrying six passengers, we decided to take it together. The problem was four of the six spaces were already taken, leaving only two beds available. The east Germans were quite adamant about the limitation of six passengers until Buck grandly offered to sleep on the couch and greased the right palms. We were a party of seven for Yokohama.

The night we were supposed to sail the ship couldn't move because the machine which raises the anchor was out of order. We were, literally, anchored in Hong Kong for three days, during which time we treated the ship as a floating hotel, returning by launch for our meals and sleeping. And we had some time to get acquainted with the other passengers: Steve, a soft-spoken young man from San Francisco, just out of India, and feeling defeated in every way; Holger and Marguerite — he somber, she jolly — a German couple looking for work; and Elfa, a giant redheaded Australian girl who smoked cigarettes in a long holder and frankly made a living by charming men. She had come from Bali.

Together, we made music every night. The East Germans were very formal and polite, but hardly friendly; they preferred to speak in German although they understood English quite well, so Holger and Marguerite had to handle most of our communication. They, as West Germans, also had a strange political relationship to the steward and crew members.

Holger was lean, tall, black mustachioed; he was interested in serious political and economic considerations of Japan. Marguerite was chubby, exuberant, interested more in the culture and language. Steve was carrying an enormous supply of Thai grass and only twenty dollars and was worried about his sexuality. Elfa worried about men, speculated on her income as a go-go dancer in Kyoto, received a cable on docking with a five-thousand-yen note attached — for her taxi to the Hilton — from an admirer. Carl planned to hitchhike up to Hokkaido and ruminate on nature. And Buck would return to his Christian halfway house in Kyoto and sell blankets. As for me, I was just going home.

By the time we docked at Yokohama, we'd become a tight-knit group, and kept in touch with each other, even reuniting from time to time at a boarding house on the edge of Kyoto. Holger had his sword cut in half by the customs police, and that proved to be an omen of his stay in Japan; he professed

176

to hate the place and the people, had been unable to find work, was living off Marguerite's earnings (she being a teacher of German and social butterfly). Buck sold few blankets but managed to spend up some savings, and was always making the rounds of Kyoto restaurants and clubs, dressed in boots and a magnificent gold-embroidered cape. Steve fell passionately in love with Kenji, who refused to leave Reiko. And Elfa, at six foot two, got used to armies of Japanese men surrounding her everywhere she went; they'd jump up and down, hands under chins, to express their desire to be as tall as she.

On my first night back in Japan, I left the others at Yokohama Station and took the train to Kamakura alone. There, I checked into the same *ryokan* where I'd stayed on my birthday the past winter. The lady of the house recognized me, and drew in her cheeks with pursed lips to indicate she found me thinner. She laid out my room perfectly, of course, drew a bath, provided me with robe and slippers, pillows and quilts, and then discreetly retreated, leaving hot tea and cookies on a tray. I slept like a baby, and dreamed my old familiar dream of being in San Francisco attempting to get back to Japan. I woke up in the middle of it anxious, terrified I would never return to Japan — woke up, and realized in a start so shocking I could feel my heart pounding, that I was *in* Japan. A single bird landed on the limb of a tree outside my window and sang me to morning. I felt relieved, grateful, comfortable.

On the second day, I contacted Kenji and other friends and fell back into the Tokyo swirl, but briefly. For my new life in Japan was mostly spent outside of the city, in a succession of places on the hilly edge of Kyoto, the ancient capital. I met a woman there, a painter named Midori, which means "green," who lived with her boy friend Shun, a graphic designer/radical student leader in a sweet one-room place by a temple where I was taken to the tea ceremony. Midori made little pictures for me, I brought her flowers; we had a very emotional though not physical relationship and I'm sure we thought each other to be angels. It was heavenly sharing that tiny room with Midori and Shun, until Shun got busted one fateful night with some Thai grass I had given him. He'd been in a car accident and was picked up for drunken driving when the baggie of weed fell out of his automobile. The police had been watching him for some time and began watching his friends' houses from parked cars. In the ensuing paranoia, Kenji came to Kyoto under an assumed name and forbade me to venture near Midori's house again, lest I be identified by the police. Thereafter Midori and I met clandestinely in small cafés near the university district where she worked in a book shop. I'd drop into the store, pretending to be an ordinary customer, and whisper the arrangement and time of our next meeting. These rendezvous usually lasted fifteen minutes and always provoked a tearful scene in which we bemoaned our friend Shun's fate and wondered how long we could go on *meeting* like this. I believe Shun served a year, and came out, from all accounts, as healthy and ambitious as ever. He even wrote me a letter apologizing to *me* for the trouble he had caused!

For a time, the best place for me to hide was in a crowd of other Americans, so I moved to a boarding-house-type hotel — except food was not offered — called simply Tani-san's. It

178

was a sprawling house, on the edge of Funaoka Park outside Kyoto Center, where all the male guests (from four to twelve) shared one enormous room with tatami floor, and a smaller side room was reserved for ladies, which was only Elfa. Elfa would let some of the guys crash on her floor after Tani-san went to sleep. We all ate at a cheap *yakisoba* joint across the avenue, and on special occasions got drunk at an expensive *sushi* parlor nearby.

Tani-san herself was a kind, small woman, an average Japanese housewife who'd found a way to make her too large home produce a secondary income. She had an eight-year-old daughter, who sometimes came downstairs for piano lessons in the parlor, and a husband who kept himself invisible upstairs most of the time. Just being in her house protected me in some ways against the anxieties of Tokyo life; my friends couldn't call me on the phone without disturbing the Tanis, for example. I spent a lot of time relaxing in parks, shrines, and temples, or talking with my friends in this mellow Western enclave.

The pace of life outside of me seemed fiercer, faster than ever all over Japan. More new products, new ideas were flying around, plus that age-old lust I felt in people's eyes, but inside of me things were more balanced, more centered. I felt in tune with my environment; it seemed completely normal and no longer exotic to be there. So I was stunned, and even confused, when Paul and Sachiko called me from New York with an urgent request that I return there.

"When are you coming home?" Paul asked. "I *am* home," I answered. But he wanted me to fly to New York to help found a magazine. I promised to take a slow boat to Vancouver or Seattle and travel on to New York by road or rail. He pressed me for an arrival date and I said, "Winter."

It was already November. Winter came down on me all at once in the darkness of Kyoto night. Tani-san's house cleared out of all but three or four hardy guests who endured sitting huddled in their sleeping bags in the unheated room, stamping their feet and drinking tea to keep warm. Snow swirled around my legs as I walked up Shijo Dori pondering my future. Nearly a year had past since the previous winter's cruel winds reddened my cheeks; I'd known, then, where I was going, but now I had no plans, no vision of what was to come except the lingering apparition of madonna and child I'd experienced at the Buddha in Kamakura. It didn't seem my fate to edit a glossy magazine from New York City, a place I can endure for only a few months at a time; but it was also clear that my work in Japan was finished, at least for the time being. I had somehow assumed I could go on wandering for years, for the rest of my life, but now friends and family were calling me back, sending money, ringing up on the phone, sending telegrams and letters. This and that needed my attention, they said; and, I knew, I was ready to see and embrace all of them again.

This frame of mind, this condition of being free to do anything, to start a new life, to live anywhere, alone or with others, is rare. Most of us have long given up and settled on one way or another to make a living, have a family, work at a business, or study at a school. Our options are limited by "practical" considerations. For me, anything I wanted to do would have been practical enough.

Actually, if I learned anything from my experience, it was

that any life one might choose to live can be made practical. I was impressed by the indefatigable spirits of human perseverance, which could live in the face of sure doom and famine. The harder thing to do, for those of us in the West whose physical survival from day to day is all but taken for granted, is to decide what's *worth* accomplishing. I waited for an inspiration, which was all I *could* do, and it came in the form of a tiny (four tables) Kyoto coffee shop called the S & M Café. Sitting there one day with Buck, keeping out of the cold and listening to Charles Mingus on the stereo, I suddenly envisioned a shop of the same size in America, which would play Japanese koto music on *its* stereo. The right place for such a personal, quiet business would be Seattle, I thought, as I'd long been taken by Seattle's charms and near bankruptcy. Seattle was caught in an economic depression years before other American cities even realized that their late-sixties prosperity was doomed; after Boeing Aircraft, the largest employer in the Pacific Northwest, laid off thousands of workers in the mid-sixties, Seattle was actually receiving relief-food shipments from Kobe, Japan. There, I realized, I could have a business which enabled me to survive on very little money in a kind and easygoing environment. Delighted with my new scheme, I promptly told all my friends in Japan, who in turn came up with the necessary stereo tapes of koto and *jamizen* music as a going-away present. They even threw in the stereo machine.

The business in Seattle, which started as a coffee shop, later turned into a Japanese bathhouse, and finally actualized itself as a bookstore and publishing company, was not an end in itself but merely a modus operandi, a piece of work to

181

accomplish, a framework in which I could carry on the business of finding a wife and having children, which is what the real holy men of India and Nepal had universally advised me to do. With my children and my shop, I would have enough distraction to send me to bed exhausted every night; I could achieve, by patient effort, both a loving family universe to which I'd retreat — the eyes of that baby in Buddha's arms shining now in my own — and a public forum through which I could meet new friends and keep in touch with the old. All these things crystalized in my mind in the space of one Charlie Mingus cut, and I made my reservations on a Norwegian freighter bound for Vancouver, British Columbia.

On the eve of my sailing from Yokohama, Kenji cooked up a party at the Aroma coffee shop in Tokyo, and I was flattered but not honestly surprised to find all my friends there waiting for me. The coffee house was closed to the public for the evening, and we ate and drank to the full. Many gifts were presented, some precious for their worldly value — like gold coins from the Meiji Era of Japan — and others for their sentimental value — like a notebook full of reminiscences, photographs, pictures, expressions of friendship and love. Predictably, the gold coins, stereo machine, samurai sword, and other stunning gifts are all gone from me now, but I still have the notebook.

We left Aroma that night in a fleet of taxi cabs to Yokohama, twelve people in all. We arrived at the ship around midnight, but she was not scheduled to sail until dawn, so all of us crammed into my little stateroom and smoked up the very last of Steve's Thai dope; and wept; and made promises of love and return. Return and return again. My friends stayed the night through and scampered off the ship as day broke and the great foghorns blew, the ship creaking into action and the Norwegian steward terrified that he'd have some Japanese stowaways. I stood on the daybreak deck in my bathrobe, barefoot, blowing kisses to the land of the rising sun.

16 THE LITTLE CITY of Powell River, British Columbia, fairly gleamed in the light of a full moon bouncing off white snowfields and heavy green forests top-heavy with ice. I stood in a pay phone booth outside the Bank of Montreal in Powell River's business district, calling a couple with whom Paul and I had stayed the winter before. Jim and Sally lived twenty miles out in the last town on the coast road.

Jim answered the phone. "Well, you old rascal, where the hell are you calling from?" he laughed.

"Powell River," I replied.

"Well, come on out. Sal's not here, she's in the hospital down there having a D and C."

184

It took me a minute to remember what a D and C is. Then I learned that the baby had apparently died inside the womb three months earlier.

"We didn't need it enough, we didn't love it enough, we didn't have the energy between us to support it," he said.

Seattle, ever gray, green, and misty, was glistening with Santa Claus in the department stores, thrift shops in the public market, bright ferries floating over Puget Sound to the islands, and logs burning in fireplaces. The holiday season had arrived, the year was about to end, and the rain never stopped.

Cathy met me at the Greyhound Bus Depot in her 1953 GMC green pickup truck with a fat joint waiting on the dashboard. Full of enthusiasm for seeing each other, we talked away the night in some bliss, while the Space Needle winked at us across the lake.

Cathy had left her partner, Lazarus, who was father of her two-year-old son. She'd left her group household and bought a place of her own, intended to calm down after years of outrageous heartbeats and study naturopathic medicine. The child, a beautiful tousled-blond boy, would live with both parents alternately.

We went on the ferry to Orcas Island, in the San Juans, where Lazarus lived in a schoolhouse with all his bookbinding equipment set up on tables. The passage was a dream of leafy groves, rich brown mud, silver skies, like a shadowplay on the garden of Eden. Lazarus served roast duck, some neighbors called for dessert — it was the nicest way I could have reentered the United States.

185

But I could not stay in Seattle, I had some business to finish in New York, so I promised to return and took the train East. Cathy and Judy gave me a basket of sandwiches and fruit to eat on the train, which passed through Montana and Minnesota, Chicago and Pennsylvania, one great old-fashioned three-day bobbing ride across the continent. They also stuck in a paperback book, the best seller of the day, but I'd never heard of it — *The Exorcist*, by William Blatty. I rode on the edge of my seat, terrified by the awesome power the book had to make a hideous situation plausible. Never in my Asian travels had I come across anything so horrifying.

New York City was like a great black cloud over my eyes. People there put their cigarette butts out in food and drinks. The mental attitude of the general public was, by and large, grim, and I had the recurrent feeling that at least half the people in the subways were clinically insane. Most, fortunately, were pale and withdrawn, but the occasional extroverts could be extremely dangerous. "Why live in a place like this?" I wondered.

Just ten months from the day I returned to the United States, my son was born by his mother's labor and love in a simple clinic in a pine wood, up at Snohomish County, Washington. The night was clear and cold, we saw stars as we drove up the freeway eighty miles per hour from Seattle. The labor was less than an hour and the baby enormous — nearly ten pounds.

He was blue as the sea and fat as the Buddha. In fact, with his puffed cheeks and eyes shut, chubby arms on chest,

186

strangely quiet and still (until the doctor administered oxygen), for a split second in time he *was* the Buddha, the absolute Perfect One bound, as he is in all of us, in flesh and bones.

And I thought, "Well, now I've seen everything."

A man doesn't own more than a single pair
    of shoes
The better to walk from end to end,
Often teasing the edge of fortune.
Big sun, big sea brought me here
And I'll find you, my love, under every tree.
A man doesn't sing for his supper till he's
    starving,
Nor walk till he can't stand still.   R.M.